Guidance and Counselling in Adult and Continuing Education

Guidance and Counselling in Adult and Continuing Education

A Developmental Perspective

RAY WOOLFE, STEPHEN MURGATROYD
AND SYLVIA RHYS

Open University Press
Milton Keynes · Philadelphia

Open University Press
Open University Educational Enterprises Limited
12 Cofferidge Close
Stony Stratford
Milton Keynes MK11 1BY, England

and

242 Cherry Street
Philadelphia, PA 19106. USA

First Published 1987

British Library Cataloguing in Publication Data

Woolfe, Ray
 Guidance and counselling in adult and continuing education: a
 developmental perspective.
 1. Personnel service in adult education
 I. Title II. Murgatroyd, Stephen III. Rhys, Sylvia
 374   LC5219

 ISBN 0 335 15986 9
 ISBN 0 335 15985 0 Pbk

Library of Congress in Cataloging No. 86–28432

Text design by Carlton Hill
Typeset by Colset Private Limited, Singapore
Printed in Great Britain by St. Edmundsbury Press Bury St. Edmunds,
Suffolk.

This book is dedicated:

by Ray Woolfe:
to his wife Adrienne; children Alexander and Clare; his mother-in-law, Winifred Small; sister-in-law, Carol Scarfi and her husband Vic; his friends, Rita and Gordon Kirkwood; and to the memory of his colleague Dennis Briggs;

by Stephen Murgatroyd:
to Canada, a new home; and to his sister, Wendy and brother, Peter;

by Sylvia Rhys:
to the memory of her father, Sydney H. Marks.

Contents

About the Authors

Ray Woolfe has worked for the past fourteen years as a Staff Tutor in Education (Senior Lecturer) for the Open University, first in Cardiff and then in Manchester. He is an Associate Fellow of the British Psychological Society and is a member of the National Executive of the Counselling Section of the BPS. He is also a member of the National Executive of the British Association for Counselling and is Chair of the BAC's Publication Group. The co-author of two major books on counselling (with S. Murgatroyd) — *Coping With Crisis: Understanding and Helping People in Need* (1982, Harper and Row) and *Helping Families in Distress: an Introduction To Family Focused Helping* (1985, Harper and Row) — he is aged 45 and is married with two children.

Stephen Murgatroyd worked for the Open University from 1975 to 1985 as a Research Fellow and Senior Counsellor, and is now Professor of Applied Psychology and Dean of Administrative Studies at Athabasca University in Alberta, Canada. Formerly Editor of *The Counsellor* and Assistant Editor of *The British Journal of Guidance and Counselling*, he has made a major contribution to counselling psychology in Britain. In addition to *Coping With Crisis* and *Helping Families in Distress* (both co-authored with R. Woolfe) he has written *Counselling and Helping* (1986, Methuen). A Fellow of the British Psychological Society, he is aged 36 and is married with two children.

Sylvia Rhys holds degrees from the University of London and University College, Cardiff, and a Diploma in Counselling. She has been a part-time tutor and counsellor in the Open University for fourteen years. Her research interests are in teaching and learning in

adults, and in staff stress in a hospital setting, and she has experience
of working with adults in a variety of training and counselling workshops. She has contributed a chapter to *Running Workshops: A Guide
for Trainers in the Helping Professions* (1986, Croom Helm).

Acknowledgements

A project of this kind involves many people and while it is not easy to single out individuals, we should particularly like to express our thanks to Sarah Fisher, Ken Giles, Camilla Lambert, Bill Law and Tony Watts for their inputs over the years to our thinking.

We should also like to thank our editor, John Skelton for his support and Christine Horner for providing such friendly and competent secretarial help. Last but not least, we owe a vast debt to the thousands of Open University students with whom we have come into contact. Without them this book might never have been written. Needless to say, responsibility for its contents rests with us alone.

Ray Woolfe
Stephen Murgatroyd
Sylvia Rhys

Introduction

The three authors of this book first came together in the 1970s under the aegis of the Open University in Wales (in Cardiff), Ray Woolfe as a Staff Tutor in Education, Stephen Murgatroyd as a Senior Counsellor, and Sylvia Rhys as a Part-Time Tutor in Social Sciences. Inevitably, as workers within an organization centrally concerned with the education of adults, each developed their expertise in this field in both the teaching and counselling of adults and the training of tutors. What brought the three together was a growing awareness of a number of common and interlinking approaches to these subjects. Perhaps the most basic was a belief in and commitment to student centred learning. This involved looking at the nature of student learning, not just as a function of what knowledge was required by a course, but also as a function of how each individual student approached and interacted with teaching methods adopted within that course. It soon became clear to us that it was just as important to consider the student's learning style as it was to examine the teacher's teaching method, if one was to gain an accurate understanding of what was involved in the enterprise of learning. This in turn led us down a number of related avenues.

One avenue was concerned with the need to acknowledge that many adult students returning to education were extremely anxious about their ability to succeed. Often many years removed from formal study, prospective and new students reported significant uncertainty and insecurity about their feelings of learning competence, ability to write essays, take notes, participate in tutorials, read economically, and a range of related study based problems. This led us towards the provision of study skill workshops for students at which anxieties could be shared, feelings explored and skills

1

developed. Another avenue focused on the idea that learning is as much an emotional as a cognitive experience. If one follows this line of reasoning, the idea of the learner as a whole person not just as a detached cognitive entity is elevated in importance. How people feel about themselves is as important as detached intellectual ability in influencing what progress they make. A recognition of this indicated to us the importance of counselling for adults; not telling them what to do but helping them to gain a better understanding of their own motivation, assets and aspirations. It could be said that we were beginning to develop a notion of the adult tutor not just as a qualified possessor of facts but as a facilitator or enabler. We were moving away from seeing learning as a product or commodity passed on from the expert to the novice, but as resulting from a process of interaction between tutor and student. In this process the latter was perceived not as an empty vessel to be filled full of facts or as a piece of blotting paper who would soak up facts but as a person with his or her own valuable experiences. Perhaps we could describe this as a 'candle to be lit' model of learning, a potential to be developed.

We reached a point, therefore, where we were soon busy running study skills sessions and doing our best to develop a way of combining students' counselling and tutorial needs. Moreover, we were applying the idea of a client centred focus to our training with tutors as well as receiving many requests to run workshops for other educational and social welfare organizations. It became clear to us, therefore, that we were not alone and that the philosophy which had brought us together was shared with many other individuals and organizations. Our interests developed further into such areas as the need for educational guidance and information services for adults and the potential implications of our work. In particular, we realized that it was necessary to think of helping students not just in terms of adapting them so that they fitted better into pre-existing systems, but actually working to change the systems so that they became more flexible and responsive to student needs. This proposition seemed to be relevant whether working with the Open University students with whom our interest began or with educational and community projects with which we became involved, concerned with people who were unemployed or lacked skills in literacy or numeracy. It also seemed relevant to traditional liberal adult education, which for all of us had represented our initial contact with continuing education, even before we joined the Open University.

This, then, is of necessity a brief background to the inspirational source and origins of this book. We hope it gives you some kind of flavour of who the authors are and where they come from — over and above the brief biographical descriptions offered at the beginning of the book. It is apparent from what has already been said that the ideas for this book were not generated overnight, but have had a long period of gestation. We think that this represents one of the book's strengths. Another is that, as we have also described, the ideas developed here arose from a long and ongoing process of bringing together theory and practice in a wide variety of settings. This has involved trying out ideas, often in the form of a workshop; reflecting with each other on that experience and using it to develop more sophisticated models of both theory and practice.

We would now like to look at the contents of the book itself so as to give you some indications of what you can expect in the pages which follow. First we should like to comment on the title: 'Guidance and Counselling in Adult and Continuing Education: A Developmental Perspective'. We have included the two terms 'guidance' and 'counselling' within the title in order to indicate the dynamic and constructive tension between the two ideas in the field of continuing education. As we indicate in a number of chapters, but particularly Chapters 2 and 6, guidance and counselling can be conceived as opposite ends of a continuum concerned with the nature of the relationship between helpers and those seeking or needing help (more in a moment about the use of this 'helping' terminology). At one end, we see guidance as involving a relatively directive form of advice and information giving. Lots of contact between adults seeking and offering advice is of this form, and we see no reason to deny its value or to suggest that it does not meet an expressed need. At the other end, we see counselling as being relatively non-directive, as being concerned with facilitating the process of decision making by the student himself or herself. This is a working definition, and like all such definitions simplifies a highly complex issue. For example, counselling normally takes place within a structure determined by the counsellor, and particularly in crisis situations can be highly directive. Nevertheless we believe that the basic distinction has a high degree of validity and offers us a useful conceptual framework through which to advance our thinking. Our aim is to explore the advantages and limitations of each approach, but not to assert the supremacy of one over the other.

Another key word in the sub-title is 'developmental'. It reflects our belief that discussions of policy making about forms of educational provision for adults really only make sense when viewed from a developmental life setting. This must contain two components, one of which is a discussion of the adult life cycle as a process of continuing change and development. As people move through the phases of adulthood, become older and have different experiences, so their learning needs and expectations change. The idea of education as a continuing or recurrent theme throughout an individual's life, a response to that life pattern, only makes complete sense when that pattern is understood as a process of ongoing transition, change and development. The second component consists of the realization that each individual life is lived through an opportunity structure. By this we mean that the social context of an individual's life heavily influences the person's expectations and aspirations. The movement through adulthood, therefore, is not one characterized by total freedom, but rather takes place against a setting which is not of the individual's choosing. The implication of this is that to understand adult development, we have to consider it not just as a psychological phenomenon, but as an interaction between psychological and sociological factors. The intention of Chapter 1 is to explore this process.

Let us, at this point, refer to the use of the terms 'helpers' and 'person seeking help' or 'person in need'. It was not easy to decide on a uniform terminology. We considered talking about 'counsellors' and 'clients', but not only did this seem to exclude those offering guidance, but both terms seemed too far removed from the likely day to day experience of many readers of this book. We toyed with the related notions of 'tutor' and 'student' (or 'student seeking help'). This terminology would be familiar to those people involved in traditional liberal adult education whom we see as one of the audiences to whom the book is directed. Indeed, these terms are used quite a lot within the book. However, it seemed to us that the exclusive use of such terminology would link the book too closely to this sector. We wanted to emphasize the notion of continuing education as learner rather than institution centred and going on in a large variety of settings over and above the archetypical educational institution. We would agree with the idea that much adult learning is of the kind which Tough describes as 'learning projects', (Tough 1976) based on personally relevant life experiences and not necessarily linked to formal education. Moreover, even that learning which is formal, now often takes place outside traditional settings. For example, the workplace is a significant forum of experience (often formally presented) about areas like planning for retirement or redundancy. Similarly Youth Training Schemes offer a massive educational and training programme, which encompasses a large number of young adults. So for all these reasons we opted against a total reliance on the terms 'tutor' and 'student' as being too restrictive. In the end we decided that the terms 'helper' and 'person seeking or needing help' represented the best compromise we could arrive at. They give some sort of sense of the kind of relationship which we address in this book and moreover, they seem to be wide enough to include all categories of readers. In our final chapter we offer an evaluative comment about our success (or otherwise) in the use of this terminology.

Because the education of adults does not necessarily take place in traditional educational settings, we have tried to offer as chapters a series of themes which cut across settings. After Chapter 1 on adulthood, the book contains three chapters which seek to offer a framework for thinking about guidance and counselling. The first (Chapter 2) is concerned to elaborate on the difference between guidance and counselling and to define what we understand by counselling. Chapter 3 looks at 'counselling in action' and attempts to develop the ideas presented in the previous chapter so that their relevance and application to the education of adults can be immediately recognized. We think that it is important for readers to read Chapter 2, before moving on to Chapter 3 or Chapter 4. Chapter 4, in a sense, can be said to take the bull by the horns. It argues that you don't have to be a counsellor (either called as such or formally trained as such) to employ the methodology and skills of counselling in your work. Indeed it goes further and suggests that whether he or she likes it or not, or even recognizes it or not, the teaching of adults itself constitutes a form of counselling. We think that you will find this chapter offers a novel and thought provoking perspective.

After the initial four chapters, the book moves on to more specific areas of application. Chapter 5 explores the subject of counselling at a distance. While this may not prima facie have been a subject many readers would particularly see as important in continuing education — apart perhaps, from the Open University — our view is that this is a long way from the truth. Counselling at a distance we think is a vitally important and growing area for a large number of persons working in the field of continuing education for adults. Chapter 6 moves on to examining what we mean by the provision of guidance and information services and the responsibility of each helper to act as an information and advice giver. Chapters 7 and 8 are concerned respectively with counselling and work; and counselling for unemployment and retirement. The former illustrates the noneducational institution base of much that passes as adult helping, while the latter addresses the important life theme of loss and grieving. Finally, we offer a short summary of our thinking, and in the process seek to explore its implications for the training of adult tutors and helpers.

Inevitably these nine chapters contain a number of recurring key themes. Some we have already alluded to: 'What is counselling?'; 'the nature of guidance'; 'adulthood as a period of transition, development and change'; 'the role of the helper as a changer of systems as well as a changer of persons'. But of course there are other important and repeated themes. One is motivation. What is it that makes adults want to learn? From where does the drive and energy derive? Another is loss, an absolutely critical notion for helpers of adults. Implicit within any life change is some sense of loss as well as possible gain. As we grow older we lose our sense of childhood, we feel less physically strong or virile, there is a sense of life as being concerned not with how old am I (time gone, as a child sees it), but of time left to live. The idea of change means that people's view of themselves and their relationships alter and often this produces further major life changes. This is the raw material with which helpers of adults work; the whole person not just the brain, the emotional not just the cognitive sector of being.

We hope that if you are a tutor of adults this book will help you to improve your practical skills and suggest to you some new ways of thinking about your work. However, the book is not intended as a detailed manual of the 'how to do it' variety. Our primary concern is to offer a set of guidelines; an integrated collection of principles together with some practical applications, which we hope will be of relevance to policy makers as well as to practitioners.

As a result of writing this book, we feel that we have become more knowledgeable and more insightful about the processes which we have described. We hope that this will also be your experience in reading it. If you have any comments to make we would be pleased to hear about them. Please write to Ray Woolfe, The Open University, 70 Manchester Road, Chorlton-cum-Hardy, Manchester M21 1PQ.

PART A

A FRAMEWORK

CHAPTER ONE

Adulthood

CHANGE IN ADULT LIFE

This book is about the counselling and guidance of adults and in this first chapter we seek to explore what is meant by the terms adult and adulthood. In our childhood, we tend to see adulthood as a rather long and unchanging plateau which concerns other people rather than ourselves. From the perspective of the adult, however, the status of adulthood may seem neither long nor unchanging. Indeed, our contention is that change in adult life is the norm rather than the exception and that it is precisely this change which generates the need for counselling and guidance.

In thinking about this idea, we find the notion of 'identity' or 'personal identity' a useful one to employ. By this we mean that every person holds a perception of themselves which consists of such things as their physical image, their psychological strengths and weaknesses and their social status. The perception represents a mix of objective and subjective factors. For instance the writers of this book have an identity as university teachers which consists of: (a) their understanding of how society values university teachers both financially and in terms of wider status; (b) what a normal career progression might look like for such an occupation; (c) what satisfactions and dissatisfactions can be expected in a normal career pattern; (d) how each of us have performed in relation to expectations, how we feel about this; and (e) what people expect university teachers to say, do and even look like — the absent-minded professor image? The mix of objective and subjective cannot be sufficiently stressed. If we underestimate the former, we lose sight of the importance of social context in defining and shaping our sense of who and what we are. If we underestimate the latter, we run the risk of being deterministic, of losing sight of the power of individuals to influence their own lives. We shall return to this theme at a number of points in the chapter.

While work roles or the lack of them may represent a significant defining influence upon personal identity, they are not of course the only ones. Our roles as spouses, parents, friends and citizens are also important shapers of identity. In each role, the individual strives to bring together external expectations with our internal conceptions of who and what we are and our place in society. The whole person can be said to represent our success or otherwise in integrating these expectations across a wide range of roles. If we do not succeed we run the risk of living in a world of fantasy, a make-believe world in which our image of ourselves does not coincide with the image of ourselves as seen by others. While fantasy can be of a mild form — for example people sometimes refer derogatorily to the woman refusing (the subjective) to accept the inevitability of advancing years (the objective) as 'mutton dressed as lamb' — it can at its extreme lead to a loss of touch with reality and to mental illness.

The ability to cope with life and its vicissitudes can be said to be dependent upon the development of a sense of personal identity which is able to reconcile internal and external factors. However, this cannot be seen as a once and for all task. While our identity provides us with some kind of core image which has a reasonably fixed basis, it cannot be so fixed that it is incapable of responding to, moving and adapting with the changing circumstances which every life involves. These usually include marriage, parenthood and illness. But the denominator which is absolutely basic to all is that of ageing, of growing up into an adult, becoming more independent, of growing older through adulthood into middle age and then into old age and finally reduced independence. In other words, our sense of self-identity, if it is to carry us through all these changes, has to be flexible enough itself to change. Another way to put this is to say that life change is best seen as a constant process and that in an emotionally healthy person, personal identity is in a constant state of change or flux. At one extreme we have the rigid person whose sense of identity is so fixed that they are unable to respond to change. At the other extreme we have the person whose core sense of identity is so weak that they find life impossibly chaotic. Hopefully most of us are somewhere in the middle for most of the time.

CAREER

The idea of objective and subjective realities has been taken up by a number of sociologists (Hughes 1937) who have employed the notion of 'career' in an attempt to produce some kind of framework which will help us to explain the changes which occur over the lifespan. The notion of the life pattern as a career implies that many people go through the same series of events, being a parent, getting a job, assuming greater career responsibility, assuming responsibility in the community, retiring etc. . But this life pattern or career can be seen to have both subjective and objective elements. Subjective refers to the personal perspective through which an individual interprets his or her life and what is happening to them. By concentrating on the subjective element of career we can gain insight into the development of personal identity (who and what we are). It is precisely the subjective element on which the counsellor seeks to focus. However, this focusing takes place against some hard objective realities, such as that a person may be unemployed or have a poorly paid job or a problematic marriage or a handicapped child or a serious illness. Concentration on the objective realities throws light upon the social structure which provides the framework and the boundaries within which individuals function. Seen in this way the typical life career can be construed as a series or sequence of roles or statuses through which an individual passes. In this process, new roles are taken on and old ones discarded. For example a person becomes a parent of a young child, then the parent of an adolescent and then a grandparent with very different parental responsibilities. Indeed, each status can be regarded as a separate role with its own set of expectations, authority and privileges. The idea of career helps to integrate the subjective and the objective. It helps us to acknowledge the social structure through which life is lived (a series of age-gradings), and yet takes into account the need to understand each individual human life from within that person's own unique frame of reference. From a slightly different vantage point, the idea of career can be said to point us in the direction of norms as regards adult life, yet to allow for the possibility that not every adult life corresponds exactly or even closely to these norms.

Let us for a while, however, focus on these norms and do so by seeking to explore what we know about adult development, particularly the field of physical and intellectual development.

PHYSICAL DEVELOPMENT

Clearly our bodies at the age of 80 are not the same as our bodies
were at 60, 40 or 20. As our perceptions of ourselves as individuals is
for most of us so powerfully influenced by our image of physical self,
it follows that the process of ageing requires the individual to engage
in a continuous process of emotional adjustment to the changing
body in which he or she lives out their life. A term like 'mutton
dressed as lamb' indicates how we perceive a person who is not prepared or is not able to accept the need for such an adjustment. A
touch more light-heartedly, who among us has never participated in
a spot of banter about their or someone else's need for rejuvenating
'monkey-gland' therapy?

But is it really as simple as this? Is life just a straightforward process
of growth from childhood into adulthood, followed by a steady
decline through adulthood? Clearly the truth is a lot more complex.
To consider this issue in more detail we have to consider the abilities
which adults possess and the way in which these are employed. Take
for example the proposition that people are at their peak in their
twenties and apply this to physical ability as expressed in sporting
achievement. Many athletes it is true do seem to reach their peak in
their twenties. However, swimmers are often said to be past their
best by the time they leave their teenage years and soccer and rugby
players are often said to compensate in knowledge about tactics what
they lose in say speed or physical reactions as they move from their
twenties into their thirties. Another conventional wisdom is that
people reach their peak sexually in their early thirties as youthful
virility is combined with growing experience of relationships.

Of course it is possible to adopt a highly scientific, experimental
perspective to the subject of physical decline during the process of
ageing. While such a perspective often raises more questions than it
answers, we think that a few 'facts' (the inverted commas are very
deliberate) may be useful. One finding is that loss of function with
increasing age does not occur at the same rate in all organs and
functions. Leaf (1973) for example suggests that taking level of
function at age 30 as equivalent to 100 per cent, by the age of 75,
brain weight has diminished to 92 per cent; nerve-conduction
velocity to 90 per cent; basal metabolic rate to 84 per cent; cardiac
output at rest to 70 per cent; filtration rate of the kidneys to 69 per
cent; and maximum breathing capacity to 53 per cent. It should be

noted, however, that it is diseases rather than gradual diminution of function which are now the main obstacle to longevity. Cross (1981) has looked at the physical changes that accompany ageing, particularly reaction time, vision and hearing. She concludes that while there is clear evidence of gradual deterioration in all three categories, this need not affect learning till the age of 75 and not necessarily even then. As for memory, the present view is that this is not a problem for the average adult so far as the potential for learning is concerned (see Beard 1967, and Puner 1974). However, this is dependent upon the initial learning being sound and the amount of new information to be stored not being too complex or large in amount. If you wish to examine the study of ageing and its effect on physical performance in more detail, we would suggest you look at units for the Open University's course 'An Ageing Population' (Open University 1979).

INTELLECTUAL DEVELOPMENT

In looking at memory, we have already introduced one aspect of intelligence and if we broaden out the discussion to include other aspects of this variable, a whole variety of interesting facts emerge. It appears that in some areas of logical problem solving such as mathematics or information technology, young adults seem able to develop skills of the highest sophistication. For instance, Bertrand Russell wrote his massive treatise *Principia Mathematica* while in his early twenties, Gary Kasparov became World Chess Champion at the age of 22, and Ruth Lawrence received a degree in mathematics from Oxford at the age of 14. In contrast, principal positions in white-collar work areas like the Civil Service, teaching and industry which clearly demand some intellectual ability are usually filled by persons in their forties, fifties and sixties. Presumably the reason for this is that experience, particularly in decision making, is somehow seen as a valuable additional asset. In the case of central government this seems to be a major priority, as most of the members of our central governments are aged over 55. In other areas like painting or literature which involve communication of moral and emotional ideas an intellectual peak may be reached only when the individual has had the opportunity to participate sufficiently in the life experiences about which they seek to communicate. We often refer to the 'period' of a painter's work or the 'developments' in a writer's style to indicate this progression. For example, William Wordsworth's poetry is located in his attempt to communicate to us his changing and more sophisticated understanding of nature and of the place of human beings in this context. As he puts it,

> I have learned
> To look on nature, not as in the hour
> Of thoughtless youth; but hearing oftentimes
> The still, sad music of humanity,
> Nor harsh nor grating, though of ample power
> To chasten and subdue. And I have felt
> A presence that disturbs me with the joy
> Of elevated thoughts. . . . (Wordsworth 1798)

Moving on to less poetic analysis of the effect of ageing upon intellectual functioning involves us getting involved in a debate between those who take a 'bearish' and those who adopt a 'bullish' stance towards changes in adult intelligence with age (Horn 1970). Broadly speaking, the latter optimistic position is that intelligence is a product of learning and so one tends to become more intelligent as one grows older. The former adopts a more pessimistic position and argues that intelligence is a physical attribute, which like all physical attributes declines with age (a maturational model). An important contribution to the debate is that of Cattell (1963) who has distinguished between fluid intelligence (Gf) and crystallized intelligence (Gc). The former is largely innate and declines with age. In contrast the latter, being largely the product of experience, increases provided mental stimulation is adequate. There is no straightforward resolution available to this controversy. A big methodological problem is that traditional measures of intelligence testing are quite simply inappropriate to the real intellectual tasks of adulthood.

One way of thinking which we find helpful in examining this issue is to conceive of intellectual functioning in adult life as closely linked to the extent of continuing exposure to intellectual stimulation. Giles and Woolfe (1981) suggest that 'the focus in this model is more on the explanation of individual exceptions to group norms, rather than to their normative behaviour'. Some interesting data supporting this point of view is provided by comparative studies of elderly men and women in Japan and the West. While studies in Western countries find little or no evidence that the intellectual level of old females is lower than that of old males, contrary results have been reported in Japan. Karasawa *et al.* (1979) suggest that 'as it is not conceivable that the biological senescent change of the brain is greater especially in Japanese females than in males, the sociocultural factors seem to be of importance'. The greater domestication and slower liberation of Japanese women means that they have had less opportunity to develop their intellectual abilities in comparison with Western women.

Our view on this discussion is that understanding of this subject is as likely to be achieved empirically in the classroom as theoretically in the laboratory the more that those who work with adults are able to demonstrate that adults want to and are able to succeed in sophisticated learning projects. We agree with Cross (op. cit.) 'that normal, healthy adults can expect to be efficient and effective learners well into old age'. What is important is that adults should feel that this is the case. Too many adults internalize a view of adulthood and of adult potential which suggests that they are on a downward slope every year after the age of 21. Helping adults is concerned to help them to question the validity of this perception, to look at the anxieties implicit within it, and to work with adults in building skills and developing the confidence which will enable them to see themselves as creative, energetic persons, capable of understanding and transforming the worlds they inhabit.

THE SOCIAL AND ECONOMIC CONTEXT OF ADULT LIFE

In discussing adult physical and intellectual development, we have been looking at one aspect of the normative context of adult life. But we would not want to leave this subject without saying something about the social and economic context of adult life and the way this affects the experience of adults. At one level such a discussion can be seen to be about the importance of work or increasingly non-paid employment in a person's life. But for many people, particularly middle-class males, occupation has traditionally provided a significant avenue for personal enhancement and the development of identity. An important feature of work is that as we get older, on the whole we assume positions of greater responsibility. We are expected more and more to be independent in our decision making and to support others. There are parallels here with the notion of the parental role. Most people reach a point where it becomes clear that they have progressed as far as they are going to in their careers. They have to come to terms with this, to adjust emotionally to the idea that younger people are passing them on the career ladder and that images of what might have been are accepted as the fantasies they are rather than being allowed to generate angry feelings in the present about opportunities lost. Finally, retirement comes, and with it a reduced income and the adjustments which this entails.

At a deeper level, however, this discussion illustrates, as we have implied all along, that it is quite incorrect to perceive individual personal identity solely as a product of individual personality, cognitive, emotional or other psychological structures. It is necessary to be absolutely clear that these structures themselves derive, at least in part, from the social and economic environment in which an individual life is located. Individuals are not free market agents exercising rational choices in a rational world. In trying to understand the attitudes or actions of individuals, we must as a prior condition acknowledge the vital importance of that individual's material conditions of existence. The issue is addressed in a book which we would highly recommend, by Peter Leonard, Professor of Applied Social Studies at the University of Warwick (Leonard 1984). He stresses the dialectical nature of the relationship between material life and individual consciousness. While accepting that states of mind (intentions) can transform material circumstances, it is generally true to say that so far as most individuals are concerned 'access to the means by which intentions can influence one's material conditions of existence is limited or enhanced by one's class, gender and ethnic minority status within the general economic structure'. Leonard proceeds to criticize psychological views of personal identity which fail to grasp the dialectical nature of this relationship. He refers on the one hand to psychoanalytic theories which emphasize the influence of the unconscious without recognizing how the unconscious derives from material conditions. On the other hand, behaviourist theories emphasize immediate material stimuli without acknowledging the influence of individual consciousness.

In understanding the idea of the dialectical relationship between human beings and society, we find it helpful to think of it in terms of 'Man in Society' and 'Society in Man' (Berger 1969). So far as the latter is concerned, human beings are socialized beings, they internalize the values of society. Society is within them. Yet what is society other than the product of past, present and anticipated future aspirations? In other words society is no more than a product of the outpourings of human activity. Thus Man is in Society. When we think about personal identity we need to conceive of it in such terms. At the very least, individuals can be said to construct an identity within the limits of a fairly well-defined opportunity structure. If helpers are not aware of the existence of such an opportunity structure, there is a danger that they perceive their work as concerned with helping under-socialized deviant individuals to adapt to a fixed and unchanging world. In our view such interventions run the risk of weakening the position of persons who seek help (Woolfe 1983).

STAGE THEORIES OF DEVELOPMENT

We would now like to draw together the subjective and the objective, the psychological and the sociological aspects of personal identity and development into a schemata for looking at personal identity and change in adult life and its implications for continuing education. In particular we would like to examine what are often known as stage theories of development. The term 'stage' is employed, because adult life is perceived as a series of steps or stages, leading from less to more complex and sophisticated interactions with the world. While everyone is seen as having the potential to move up the hierarchy of stages, not everyone succeeds. Within this tradition the notion of the 'life-cycle' is an important organizing principle and the work of Erikson (1950) and Havighurst (1953) has been of particular pioneering importance. Havighurst refers to the idea of adults being faced with a series of 'developmental tasks'. In each age period, a problem or barrier has to be overcome before the individual can progress towards personal and social maturity. Failure to resolve the problem results in unhappiness, disapproval by society and difficulty with future tasks. Havighurst sees adulthood as containing three developmental tasks:

(a) *Early adulthood* (18–30 years): the task includes selecting a marriage partner, learning to live with that person, starting a family and bringing up young children and starting off in an occupation.
(b) *Middle age* (35–60 years): the task includes achieving civic and social responsibilities, maintaining an economic standard of living, assisting one's children to become adults and adjusting to physical changes.
(c) *Late maturity* (65+ years): the task includes adjusting to

decreased physical strength and the prospect of death, as well as adjusting to retirement and reduced income.

The list of tasks indicates yet again the complex interrelationship of physiological, psychological, social and economic changes in the life of each individual. Huberman (1974) suggests that there is a striking correlation between the tasks as outlined by Havighurst and the type of educational courses followed by adults. Vocational courses are dominated by younger people and by women released from child rearing while courses in community affairs and cultural topics tend to be followed by the middle-aged. We shall return shortly to a further discussion of Huberman's work.

Erikson's work is Freudian in inspiration and involves a developmental theory comprising stages of ego development from infancy to old age. Each stage, like the tasks in Havighurst's model, involves a personal crisis, whose resolution determines the future development of the personality as well as the individual's reactions to people and objects, his or her success in adapting to internal and external demands and the person's perception and evaluation of themselves. Erikson sees adulthood as containing three stages, each with its own crisis or turning point: *intimacy v isolation*; *generativity v stagnation*; and *ego integrity v despair*. The first crisis is concerned with the need to establish intimate relationships which involve a fusing of identity with other people — as for example in marriage. The second crisis involves the need to be creative and to give of oneself to other people — for example to one's children, friends, colleagues and the community generally. If this does not happen, the result is stagnation and self-absorption which makes that much harder the overcoming of the final challenge which involves coming to terms with life as finite and one's one and only life.

Erikson would see what has come to be referred to in popular mythology as 'mid-life crisis' as resulting from a feeling of loss of purpose and failure to resolve the second crisis. Neugarten (1977) invites us to think about the period of middle age as involving us in the process of coming to think about life in terms of 'time left to live'. If this generates a feeling of time wasted or underachievement or worthlessness, then the potential for crisis might exist. Emotional problems in old age would arise if the individual sees life as a chapter of failures and missed opportunities. In thinking about Erikson's model we must avoid the danger of interpreting it literally. Erikson is not saying that each individual experiences each crisis at a particular point of time. That is far too mechanical an interpretation of a model which is meant to be a heuristic guide to our thinking. Moreover, the model cannot be proved in any scientific sense. While some people may experience life as a series of crises, others seem to go through life, often despite serious vicissitudes, without any subjective sense of going through the kind of crises outlined by Erikson and yet without becoming soured or dispirited or lonely or uncreative.

IMPLICATIONS FOR THE EDUCATION OF ADULTS

Helpers who work with adults are concerned to help them to resolve developmental tasks and problems so as to move to higher stages of development. That is the clear implication of the stage model. Loevinger (1976) makes this quite explicit. She offers a hierarchy based on the work of Erikson and involving stages from 'presocial' (infancy) to 'integrated' (maturity). Each stage has its own preoccupations, interpersonal style, and ways of thinking and problem solving. She sees the educator as helping individuals to achieve the goal of integration. At the lower level stages, education is viewed as a product, something one gets in school, while at a higher 'conformist' stage, education is valued for its practical usefulness. Higher up the hierarchy, at the 'conscientious' stage, education is seen as having a potential for personal enrichment, while at the highest stages described as 'autonomous' and 'integrated' education is seen in terms of creativity and self-fulfilment. Each stage is linked to a specific cognitive style, a theme taken up by Allman (1983) who perceives adult development as linked directly to cognitive development, and as made possible by increasingly complex ways of thinking about complex issues which are part of the experience of adulthood. 'What people think and how they think emerges from people's transactions or interactions with their social and historical contexts.' Experience changes our ways of thinking and feeling.

Seen in this way the role of the helper in helping people to advance to higher levels of understanding is intimately linked to helping them to understand how they have become who and what they are. This theme has been developed by writers such as Freire (1972) and Mezirow (1979) who have seen education as the means by which people come to perceive, interpret, criticize and, most importantly, transform the worlds in which they live. Freire refers to this process as 'conscientization', whereby people are helped not just to understand their past but to develop a vision of the future. A crucial part of the process is that the helper – person being helped relationship is altered so that it ceases to become one of active knower and passive receiver. Mezirow refers to the very similar idea of 'perspective transformation' with reference to re-entry programmes for women into education. He describes how the helper helps adults to become critically aware of taken for granted assumptions about their social roles and expectations and habituated ways of thinking and feeling developed within these roles. Mezirow sees adults as possessing the facility for 'reflexive thinking' or 'critical reflectivity', an ability to tolerate ambiguity and contradiction and that this has major implications for the education of adults and the practice of educators. The theory is radical or critical because it encourages learners to look at how their understanding of themselves is influenced by their educational experiences. This may well lead them to question taken for granted assumptions about education such as those pertaining to the nature of the teacher-student relationship.

But of course, this is all highly theoretical. What does it mean in, say, the 'nitty-gritty' area of course provision? Cross (1981) attempts to answer this question by describing each life cycle phase as having three characters: (a) 'marker events' such as leaving home, getting married, being promoted etc.; (b) 'psychic tasks' as discussed by Erikson and others and corresponding to the question of *what* adults need to learn at each phase; and (c) 'characteristic stance' such as building for the future, concern for order and stability, levels of nurturing and assertiveness, etc. . These correspond to the question *how* do adults learn? So for example in the words of Cross, 'the younger learner's concern (age 19–34) about order and setting long-range goals suggests a fairly aggressive search for goal-specific education, a willingness to compete in order to "make it", and perhaps a willingness to conform to certification and degree criteria in order to advance career goals.' In contrast, the older learner might well be turned off by such an aggressive, competitive stance. He or she would be more likely to respond favourably to analytical discussion rather than acquiring new information and would 'be less interested in conforming to externally imposed regulations in the interests of having the learning accepted by others'.

Huberman attempts to relate continuing education to a 'cycle of adult concerns', which he describes in the following way:

(a) *Focusing one's life (18 to 30):* Adolescence is concerned with the task of establishing a relatively stable psychological identity, whereas early adulthood is concerned with the social side of personal identity: finding a spouse, a job, a community in which to live, a job to develop. Participation in adult education is largely professional and vocational. The person's need for counselling and guidance is therefore, likely to lie within this sector of activity and concern.

(b) *Collecting one's energies (30 to 40):* A more stable period involving a growth in skill and experience, an income increase, a preoccupation with child rearing and a general moving out from family participation to community participation. Participation in education continues to be instrumental, a means to an end and vocational and professional courses continue to dominate. However, Huberman suggests that there is a heightened interest in group activities and in expressive forms of education, ends in themselves such as learning a foreign language, painting or musical appreciation.

(c) *Exerting and assuring oneself (40 to 50):* Here the individual's involvement in the community is at its height, with a big interest in civic and social affairs and politics. Work may also be a major preoccupation. While educationally, civic affairs and cultural subjects are important, a new development is the presence of large numbers of women — freed from child rearing — attempting to establish new careers, as well as some men seeking career change. Educationally, this is reflected in a growing number of courses concerned with wider opportunities for women, discovering one's hidden abilities, running a small business, making decisions etc. . The need for counselling in supporting this process is clear and apparent.

(d) *Maintaining one's position and changing roles (50 to 60):* A plateau is reached in terms of social influence and economic productiveness. Huberman suggests that ego concerns turn inwards and thought replaces action, reflected educationally in the high enrolment in adult education of this group in courses in literature, philosophy and religion.

(e) *Deciding whether and how to disengage (60 to 70):* A decreasing interaction between the individual and society. This is characterized educationally by an interest in less creative, more contemplative and cultural courses, such as international relations, cultural tourism and economic and political affairs.

(f) *Making the most of disengagement (70 to 80):* The concerns of old age are generally those of reduced financial means and health, and increased dependence on others. Educationally the move towards interpretive and aesthetic courses of study continues.

Just as Erikson's model or any other model is to be taken as a working framework, so the same comment applies to Huberman's paradigm. The idea of disengagement, for example, is not one which should be accepted uncritically. On the contrary, it deserves to be challenged. It adopts rather a pessimistic view of the ability of older people to relate to and to contribute to the community of which they are part. Moreover in the years since Huberman's work was published, Western industrial societies, notably Britain, have experienced major economic disruption and change resulting notably in high levels of unemployment among many people. This has created a large body of young people who may never seriously expect to have a career and it has stimulated the idea of earlier retirement, so that jobs can be shifted from older to younger persons. As high unemployment seems likely to be an endemic feature of our society, we would do well to consider the validity of paradigms like Huberman's which give a central role to the experience of work in the shaping of personal identity and the demand for particular programmes of continuing education for adults. Nor are changes confined just to unemployment. Views on marriage and the family seem to be altering with some rapidity and there is an increasing challenge to the notion of women as the providers of unpaid domestic labour during the child rearing phase. In addition, the model takes little account of the life-style of cultural minorities such as homosexuals. While these provisos suggest that the picture is a changing one, they also suggest that the need for counselling for adults continues to grow.

THE MOTIVATION OF ADULTS TO LEARN

These concerns are well illustrated from the authors' own involvement in the Open University. For many younger students, particularly men, the motivation for study is primarily extrinsic or instrumental. By this we mean to suggest that students are, to put it baldly, in it for what they can get out of it. An Open University course of study is seen as a means to a career change or to promotion in work. For older students on the other hand, courses are often undertaken primarily for more intrinsic or expressive reasons, i.e. interest in the course itself is a sufficient reason for doing it. It is a useful way to spend time available. A third group of students, often women in their thirties or forties, begin to study seriously because they have the time available as children grow up and wish to do something interesting and in the process explore their own interest and potential as persons. What often happens, however, is that in the process of learning things about themselves, students find that their perceptions of themselves change and with it their aspirations and expectations. So, for example, many women students become aware of their own intellectual abilities and gradually begin to focus on perhaps a particular career. Open University courses are gradually selected more and more for their value in sharpening up this objective as motivation becomes increasingly extrinsic. In contrast, a fourth type of student may begin to study with primarily extrinsic motives, but may increasingly become attracted to the idea of studying courses as something of intrinsic interest and value in its own right. Perhaps you could spend a moment reflecting on your own institution and students (if you are a tutor of adults). Consider on the one hand the assumptions made by the institution about the students' motivation as reflected in the provision of courses, and on the other hand the nature of student motivation as you understand it and the way this relates to the stage they have reached in their personal and career development.

We would offer the following suggestions about types of motivation and the way in which they might be reflected in particular sorts of courses. This list is intended to offer a flavour of what we are getting at; it is not intended to be exhaustive:

(a) the need to further vocational competence — reflected in post-experience courses in science or technology or education for example;

(b) the need to develop new job patterns — reflected in courses on vocational preparation, conversion courses, courses on self-assessment and decision making, starting a small business, running a cooperative enterprise etc.;

(c) the need to cope with status passages such as becoming a parent or reaching retirement. This is reflected in the Open University, for example, by courses on the one hand for

new parents such as 'The First Years of Life', 'The Pre-
School Child', and 'Childhood 5–10', and on the other hand
by a course on 'Retirement';

(d) the need to continue one's learning as an adult — this is
reflected in the traditional domain of much liberal adult
education in Britain which is concerned with the provision
of courses in literature, music, art, foreign languages,
sociology, economics etc.;

(e) the need to express oneself as a member of the community,
reflected in courses on such topics as consumer rights,
public speaking, chairing a committee or developing negotiating skills.

Below we have produced a table of the kind of students we have been
discussing within the Open University context. Perhaps this will aid
your thinking about your own institution. How far do your students
deviate from this pattern? What are the implications of this model for
the practice of counselling adults about their needs?

Table 1.1   AGE and MOTIVATION

Age of students	Gender	Motivation
20s and 30s	Predominantly male	Education as a vehicle for career change, development, promotion or enhancement. Motivation is extrinsic/ instrumental.
30s and 40s	Predominantly female	Education as a way of doing something inter-esting. Intrinsic/expres-sive motivation. However, there is also a desire to find out some-thing about oneself, perhaps as a vehicle for developing a career.

		Extrinsic/instrumental motivation.
50s and 60s	Male and female	Education as an interesting field of activity in its own right. An interesting and valuable way of using leisure. Motivation is intrinsic/expressive.
30s and 40s	Predominantly male	Education as vehicle for promotion — extrinsic/instrumental motivation is gradually superseded by a growing interest in education as an interesting field in its own right. Motivation now becomes more intrinsic/expressive.

Once again, it has to be stressed that the table (model) is an abstraction from reality (a guide to our thinking); it does not claim to be an exact, literal representation of reality. It assists our thinking, because it guides us towards a deeper understanding of the adult developmental basis which underlines the specific issues which adults bring for discussion to helpers. While the latter have always to be sensitive towards the particular concern brought by each individual, these concerns can be understood in terms of a number of general questions about adulthood such as (a) how old is this person?; (b) is this a man or woman?; (c) what is his or her work experience?; (d) what are his or her expectations of work?; (e) how are these expectations satisfied?; (f) what are his or her expectations of family life?; (g) how are these expectations satisfied?; (h) what are this person's motives for studying or for wanting to study?. In other words the helper works to locate the individual in the kinds of models of adult career development to which we have referred, seeking to understand both the objective structure of the individual's life and the latter's subjective perception of this structure.

LEARNING ABOUT SELF

So far we have attempted in this chapter to establish:

(a) that adult life (adulthood) is a period of great change;
(b) that it is possible to present a framework around which this change can be explored. Thus we can see adulthood as a career or as the process of moving through the life-cycle;
(c) that these changes generate the energy or the motivation for adults to continue their education;
(d) by looking at this motivation, we are able to understand why adults choose one type of course of action rather than another.

In the final section of the chapter we would like to proceed a little further by raising the question of why change is unsettling and why it places a premium on the provision of counselling support. To some extent we have already answered these questions implicitly, but we should now like to address them in a more explicit fashion. People seek change for a variety of reasons: because they are bored with their existing patterns of existence, because they gradually develop a new objective to work towards, because they gain flashes of insight, because they seek excitement and find the process of change itself is pleasurable. Some of these are 'carrot'-type reasons, others smell more of the 'stick'; some are short term, some make sense only when seen over a much longer time perspective. Precipitative desire for change may be internal, for example a growing awareness that one is dissatisfied with one's life, or it may be external, for example redundancy or the birth of a handicapped child. People do not respond in the same way to the same events. Therefore, coping with change is to be seen not as referring to whether or not a person is successful in their response, but rather as relating to what strategy is being employed to deal with the situation. We have developed this point further in our books *Coping With Crisis* (Murgatroyd and Woolfe 1982) and *Helping Families in Distress* (Murgatroyd and Woolfe 1985). It follows that when we talk about helping a person to cope with change, what we are talking about is helping that person to find a coping strategy that will suit them. Such a strategy may be confrontative (attack the problem), or anticipative (developing an awareness of how to deal with likely contingencies), or re-definitive (coming to perceive change in a slightly different way than hitherto), or withdrawal (removing oneself from the situation in some way, physically or emotionally). The point is that the helper's task is to help the individual to cope with the anxiety of change or perhaps its normlessness. The feelings that change generates for many people are of uncertainty, anxiety, loss, perhaps excitement and casting around for new understandings, life focus and direction. This is the raw material with which helpers work. But whatever an individual's motivation to change, learning about a subject cannot be divorced from learning about self. Adult students learn about their anxieties about failure; they learn about how much more competent they are as learners than they had originally imagined; they learn that they are more interesting people than they had once thought; they learn that they are good/not so good in groups; they learn that they don't accept criticism very well; they learn that they are least as bright as their spouse; they learn that they are more ambitious for themselves than they had imagined. The list is of course endless. But what it means is that the very nature of continuing education for adults itself places adult learners in the position of facing up to what may be, for many people, very new and frightening feelings. Even pleasure can create anxiety. For example, the adult student who discovers that there is a whole new world of people outside the rather boring marital relationship through which life has traditionally been lived. That realization may give hope and pleasure and excitement, but its potentially unsettling effect can also create anxiety about the student's ability to accept his or her present world. This reinforces the point that people do not seek to require help only when life is seen as a mess, or when there is a large problem or crisis, or when they are experiencing severe emotional pain. Helpers are also concerned to help people choose between different options which may each have their own attractions.

LOSS AS A CHARACTERISTIC OF ADULT LIFE

What the last couple of paragraphs illustrate is that change in adult life involves the potential for loss as well as for gain. Loss is a subject with which counsellors are much concerned, loss not just in the sense of that which results from death, but also from a variety of other aspects of adult life. These include (a) loss resulting from divorce or separation; (b) loss resulting from unemployment or redundancy or the failure by a young person to get a job — the loss here is the loss of an expected occupational structure; (c) loss to parents of an anticipated ideal child when a handicapped child is born, or just loss of freedom when any child is born; (d) loss of body image as a result of limb amputation or mastectomy; (e) loss of friends as a result of moving house; (f) loss of childhood as one grows older — a sense of loss of virility; (g) loss of one's children as they grow up and leave home (the 'empty nest' syndrome). Perhaps you would like to think for a moment about the losses you have experienced in your own adult life. Perhaps you could jot them down on a bit of paper. Perhaps you are surprised by the size of your list or maybe your list is very small.

Our expectation would be that you may be surprised by the size of your list and that this reflects the fact that adulthood as a period of change is characterized by endemic loss. Change in fact consists of both loss and gain. We see the two as tied together in some sort of symbiotic process. Indeed, it is the very fact of loss which often generates the motivation towards change. It is the fact of being made redundant or the realization that the children are growing up or the feeling that life won't stand still just because a tragedy has occurred that pushes people towards change and new learning. Loss, therefore, can be said to contain the seeds for regeneration or personal change in adult life. The reason loss has such a powerful effect on individuals lies in our need as human beings for attachment to spouses, friends, children, parents, jobs, communities and causes. It is these attachments which offer us the opportunity for intimacy. Yet they also describe for us in a nutshell the central paradox of human life: that we want to achieve our potential as separate individual adults and yet that this has to be reconciled with our equally strong need to be intimate, to be attached, to belong. The elegance of adult education is that it allows the potential for both these aspects of human need to develop in harmony with one another. Nevertheless if a loss of attachment does occur, the task of filling the gap is not a simple one of replacing one thing with another. We are all aware of the value of time in helping us to cope with the losses experienced in adulthood. During this period of time, the individual classically goes through a process of grieving (bereavement) for what is lost. We would like to articulate this process for you. As we do so, ask yourself how far each stage in the process might be reflected in the motivation of students to engage in continuing education and what continuing education offers or might offer in the way of helping the individual to work through the process.

To cope successfully with loss, it is necessary for the person to work through a process of bereavement, a process of grieving for what is lost (see Parkes 1972; Murgatroyd and Woolfe 1982). This characteristically involves a number of stages. An initial phase of shock is accompanied by disbelief and denial, by which individuals protect themselves from the enormity of what has happened. Predominant feelings here may be of anger, sadness and guilt. This is followed by a period of searching for what is lost, a search sometimes in a physical sense but often in the mind and imagination. This leads, perhaps inevitably to a stage of finding (or to put it more precisely, re-finding). The person discovers what they have lost in their imagination. Thus the spouse of the deceased person after an initial phase of denial now constantly talks about the person or the redundant worker leaves the house at the same time every morning as he or she used to when in work. Emotional health cannot, however, be based forever on a fantasy life, and eventually there is a re-loss as a realization dawns that substitution is not the same as the real thing. This leads through a process of adaptation, of finding new ways to cope with the situation to a final stage of acceptance, of emotional burial in which the dependency on what is lost disappears.

Continuing education can be seen as an important aspect of the process of grieving, whereby individuals come to terms with the losses in their lives. It helps by (a) giving information; (b) helping to develop new skills; (c) providing a forum for social interaction; (d) filling time; (e) offering a sense of direction and purpose; (f) offering a sense of shared enterprise. Most important, it offers the opportunity to develop new strategies for coping with change. Perhaps you can think of other ways in which continuing education can be said to help adults cope with the losses involved in adult life.

CONCLUSION

Our contention is that if adulthood is seen in the way we have described, as a period of immense change, the need to explicitly express the counselling function in adult and continuing education is strong and powerful. What we are suggesting is that every tutor should also think of himself or herself as a counsellor. Many, of course, already think of themselves in this way. It may be, however, that institutions should consider the desirability of appointing more persons specifically as counsellors or at least recognizing the counselling function in the terms and conditions of service of all tutorial staff. We hope that the discussion about the nature of adulthood in this chapter has helped to provide a basis for this contention.

What is Counselling?

CHANGING AND HELPING

The first chapter looked at human development in terms of changes which take place as we move on our personal journeys through life, and the need we have to develop a sense of personal identity which is capable of responding to the changing circumstances which are part of every life. It can be useful to conceptualize changes in terms of stages, such as those by Erikson and Huberman which were referred to in Chapter 1. At different stages different roles and different concerns predominate, and different dimensions of our lives assume particular importance. For example, family life may be of special significance to us in our thirties, while in our seventies, health and financial circumstances may preoccupy us.

This concept of stages is based on the notion of progression through the life-cycle. But all the changes which we experience do not necessarily accord with normative development over time. We also experience changes which can be regarded as introducing discontinuity into the pattern of life stages. Examples include divorce, death of husband or wife, redundancy, the onset in early life of physical disability. We need resources and the ability to use them flexibly in order to cope with these transitions, as well as with the changes which accompany movement through life stages.

Our sense of self and of our own value depend on the presence of others and our interactions with them. As time passes and we gain more experience of life, we alter our ways of doing, thinking and feeling to a greater or lesser degree, and in a sense change as people. At the same time people around us are changing, and so are our physical environments. Some of the changes in the self and the environment with which we have to find ways of coping — whether these are of the developmental or the transitional type — we may experience as of a relatively minor nature, involving only small modifications in the ways in which we cope with ourselves and others. Other changes we may experience as major upheavals in our lives, retirement, and loss of a marriage partner, for instance, often fall into this category.

Most changes we cannot cope with successfully by simply juggling the contents of our heads and recognizing at a cognitive level only that things are different, although there may be those who would say that this is possible. Change usually involves placing ourselves in a new relationship to ourselves, i.e. regarding ourselves differently as persons, and/or placing ourselves in a new relationship to the world, i.e. altering ways in which we regard and interact with our environments (Smail 1980). Such re-positioning, whether on a major or minor scale, may well have its difficulties. We may go through a form of grieving for the familiar, as suggested in Chapter 1, and change is likely to involve a feeling of risk and uncertainty. We have never thought of ourselves in quite this way before, and/or we have never related to others on exactly these terms previously. We have to learn how to cope with the unfamiliar until it becomes part of our way of living.

This process of re-adjustment is necessary in whatever terms we view the change. Some changes in our lives, such as acquiring paid employment after months of searching, may be welcome; others, such as redundancy, may not be welcome. Some changes, such as retirement, may be expected; others, such as family bereavement may come without warning. Once one change has taken place it may lead on to others. For example, acquiring a job may result in increased economic means, learning new skills, opening up of a new network of friends and acquaintances, changes in social life, and so on.

How great is the feeling of risk and uncertainty that is associated with any particular change varies from one individual to another. For example, joining a social club may be regarded as a relatively minor undertaking by one person, but to someone else who experiences difficulties in relating to strangers it may be a major step in his/her life. We do not always possess a wide enough range of resources to cope satisfactorily with a particular situation, or perhaps we do not know how to apply those resources which we have, and feel over-whelmed by life.

Change, then, is a familiar feature of our lives. Sometimes we feel we can take it in our stride, and sometimes we find it imposes strains on us. We recognize that it takes place in ourselves and in others. Helping one another in our daily lives is also a generally accepted feature of social existence. Human distress arises very often out of human commerce, but so also does help to cope with that distress. Such helping may be with routine daily tasks of living, such as assisting someone off a bus. We also help one another to tackle times of change in our lives, changes of minor and of more fundamental importance to us.

Most of us take part at one time or another, on an informal basis in our private lives, in the process of giving help to and receiving help from different people in a variety of settings. This may happen, for example, in the course of interactions with members of our family at home, with friends and relatives in their homes, with fellow workers at our workplace, with those sharing in the same leisure activities as ourselves in clubs, and so on. In addition, many of us are also involved in giving and receiving help on a more formal basis in our public lives. For example, there are many people — especially in service industries, like bus conductors and shopkeepers — who in the course of their jobs help others with routine tasks of living. Society appoints a variety of professional helpers, such as social workers, teachers, and nurses, whose job it is to help others with particular aspects of their lives. Often they are seeking to help others to cope with changes, such as the desertion of a family by a parent, acquiring additional academic qualifications, and coping with severe illness.

The helping process as such still tends to be taken very much for granted in both informal and formal settings. While many professional helpers have received some training, even this is unlikely to have included paying much, if any, attention to the actual process of helping as a topic in its own right. In some quarters it is beginning to be recognized that this dimension of communication is both complex and important. For example, in nursing there is an increasing recognition of the importance of the psychological and emotional needs of patients as well as of their physical needs, and courses are being developed around the emerging, 'nursing process'; see, for example, the Open University Course, 'A Systematic Approach to Nursing Care: An Introduction' (1984).

Those who want to learn about the helping process in some detail usually have to seek out a course in counselling. This is a profession in which the helping process forms a central part of training. Counsellors study, for example, different ways of communicating verbally

and non-verbally, the assumptions people make when they communicate, and how personal values affect what we say and do and how
we think.

Trained counsellors are found in many different walks in life. Some
teachers, some of those who give educational guidance, some who
help others in work, and some who help people to cope with
unemployment and retirement — the topics covered in this book —
have undertaken this training. Some social workers similarly are
trained in this way, and so are certain voluntary workers, such as
marriage guidance counsellors. A few people set themselves up in the
occupation of counselling as such to help people with personal
problems in living. (Not all people, however, who describe themselves as counsellors have undergone training; in this chapter the
term counsellor applies only to those who have undertaken a close
study of the helping process.)

A basic assumption of this book is that each of us, whether seeking
to assist others on an informal basis and/or in some public capacity,
could improve our help by critically examining the nature of the
helping process, and by relating what we learn to the way in which
we go about seeking to help others. Good intentions in themselves do
not make the help which springs from them automatically constructive for the person in need, and indeed it is possible by misplaced
interventions to hinder another person's efforts to cope with change.
Being more fully acquainted with the complexities of the helping process does not guarantee that we always help another person in the
way most appropriate for him/her, but it increases the chances of this
being so. There is no need for us all to become counsellors in order to
be better helpers, but by looking at counselling we can improve our
understanding of basic helping skills; and it is to the counselling
process that attention is now turned.

AIMS OF THE COUNSELLING PROCESS

There have been many attempts to define the term 'counselling'. For
example, Murgatroyd (1982) has listed 23 definitions, and the list is
not claimed to be exhaustive. This multitude of definitions is perhaps
not surprising in view of the complexities of the process of helping
another human being, and the number of different approaches to it
which are possible. It does seem safe to say, however, that there is a
general theme running through most, if not all, definitions, and that is

that counselling is about helping people to help themselves to live their lives more effectively. It is variously described in terms of, for instance, '... assisting individuals towards responsible independence, development of maximum potential, or self-actualization' (Arbuckle 1967); 'helping other people to grow towards their personal goals, and to strengthen their capacities for coping with life' (Brammer 1979). We can say that counselling is about life and about how to choose to live it within the constraints of personal limitations and those of the social structure and physical environment in which we are placed. It is about the 'nitty-gritty' of human existence, about people as thinking, feeling and doing beings.

Counsellors in their role as skilled helpers are not sentimental idealists. It is important to make this point because problems in living are rarely open to solutions in the sense that they disappear completely. Counsellors cannot work miracles, or bring about cures for ills in the lives of others. But counsellors may be able to help others to improve the quality of their lives by assisting them to become better equipped to cope more effectively with one or more aspects of the process of living. For example, it may perhaps be that someone in need does not recognize creative talents already possessed and which might be employed constructively in, say, retirement; or if another person increased his/her store of knowledge, perhaps of the law, this might be a means of finding some practical ways of coping with difficult neighbours; or perhaps learning how to use resources better, such as becoming more assertive, might be a way for another individual to cope more effectively with difficult family relationships. The extent to which people can be helped to improve the quality of their lives, however, is constrained by the nature of the resources people possess and by their environmental circumstances, both personal and impersonal. Lack of education, physical or mental handicap, low income, poor housing conditions, pressing family commitments, an unhappy marriage, are all examples of factors which may restrict the number of options open to people in difficulties.

Hopson (1982) has suggested that there are four possible strategies for dealing with problems in living. It may be that a person in difficulties can do something to change a situation, at least to some extent. Another possibility is that a person might change the self in some way to adapt to the situation better. Alternatively, a person might decide that the most suitable course of action is to get out of the situation altogether. The fourth strategy is to stay with the situation and to develop ways of living with it. Sometimes a combination of these strategies might be employed. For example, if a person is unhappy in his/her paid employment, and this is wholly or in part due to difficulty with some aspect of the working conditions, then approaches to the management either directly or through a trade union may be made with a view to bringing about some changes. It may be, however, that this course of action involves taking a new view of the self and becoming more assertive in the face of authority and more confident in one's ability to act in this way. Alternatively, learning to be more assertive might of itself be a way of coping with the situation more effectively if the difficulties involve interrelationships with fellow workers. Perhaps the difficulties are such that changing jobs seems to be the only appropriate way in which to act. Perhaps, however, it is not possible to do this, and finding ways of living with the difficulties would appear to be the only course of action open.

Whichever of these four courses a person seeking help selects, it involves that person in change. It involves giving up a situation or a way of coping with a situation which is familiar, and taking a new direction. It may be that an individual *acts* differently in connection with some aspect of his/her life, and/or *thinks* about that aspect of life along different lines, and/or *feels* differently about it. Usually doing, thinking and feeling are all involved to some extent, because in all of us they are so closely interconnected. For example, Jennifer complains of being depressed and part of the reason is that she feels she cannot get any further in her career because she is not intelligent enough to gain qualifications. With encouragement, she attends a 'return-to-learning' study course and finds that she is able to play a constructive part in discussions and has some ideas to put down in writing. Having gained a little more confidence in herself she then takes a decision to enrol on a course leading to the qualifications which she needs.

If we take new directions this is likely to involve relationships with others, and there are likely to be 'knock-on' effects. This is because we are all part of society, and human life is socially negotiated. When we change, then this affects in some way the nature of our relationships with other people, and when other people change, this affects in some way their relationships with us. In the example above, a colleague with whom Jennifer worked was impressed by the decisions Jennifer had made, and it increased her respect for her. The following year she decided to follow Jennifer's example, and the two found they could help each other by sharing learning experiences.

People do not usually adopt overnight new ways of coping in the long term with problems in living. It normally takes place step by step as an individual thinks about a situation, tries out different ways of dealing with it, and eventually finds and becomes accustomed to a more appropriate way of acting, and/or thinking, and/or feeling. It is possible that there may be subsequent repercussions of a positive or negative nature, and then ways have to be found of coping with these.

A crisis may well be a catalyst for long-term learning. Counsellors sometimes help people to cope with problems in which there is a need to find some way of taking action quickly in order to ameliorate the effects of a situation on them. What a counsellor offers in addition to immediate assistance is help to people to grow through a crisis, to use the experience as an opportunity for learning how to increase resources so that they are better equipped to cope with change in the future (Murgatroyd and Woolfe 1982). Not all people who seek help when in difficulties, however, may wish to avail themselves of this offer. They may regard a particular crisis as an end in itself to be put behind them as rapidly as possible. An individual cannot be compelled to accept long-term help, and counsellors have to be able to accept that offers of help may sometimes be rejected.

METHODS IN COUNSELLING

How do counsellors set about helping other people to help themselves? What sort of tasks do they see as part of the helping process, and how do they put them into practice? This section looks at these aspects of the helping process in general terms. The next chapter will discuss them in greater detail.

It is the emphasis on non-direction which distinguishes counselling from many other types of help given to adults, both informally and formally. For example, in their private lives some people see helping relatives and friends in terms of taking over and 'doing things for' another person, so that that person has to do very little in the way of acting or thinking or feeling for him/herself. Sometimes on a temporary basis this may be a highly appropriate way of helping a person in acute distress. But, if this is the only form of help offered at a time of change in personal life, it may hinder rather than help because it is unlikely to assist a person in distress to look at an issue fully, and may encourage that person to avoid accepting responsibility to

do so; it may prevent that person from trying out new ways of thinking, feeling and acting; and it assumes that the helper knows what are
the needs of and the best course of action for the person in difficulties.
Counsellors may offer support and a shoulder to lean on until a
person in distress has enough strength to start work on the counselling process, perhaps, for instance, by encouraging emotional dis-
charge of strong and confused feelings which have been 'locked up'
internally, but after these are released it may then be appropriate to
encourage that person to start looking at them with a view to
becoming less frightened and overwhelmed by them.

Those who are being helped are encouraged to play an active part
in the helping process. This is essential if they are to learn how to help
themselves. A counsellor does not tell another person what decisions
to make, or issue instructions about how to set off in a new direction,
and which direction to take. A counsellor helps other people to do
this for themselves. There is no place for such phrases as 'If I were
you, I would . . .', or 'What you need to do is . . .'. If information is
given it is not done in such a way that it strongly influences a person
to act, feel or think along particular lines. A counsellor seeks to provide information in as unbiased a way as possible in order that a
person in need may be better equipped to weigh up a situation and
choose between alternative courses of action for him/herself. Sometimes a counsellor provides help which might be described in terms
of teaching or guidance, but again this is geared towards helping the
person in need to achieve greater autonomy. For instance, it may
well be necessary to help an individual to learn how to practise
different skills, such as ways of analysing a problem, and of becoming
more self-aware.

It is, however, important to recognize that it is very difficult, if not
impossible, to be completely non-directive. Each of us has a set of personal values and theories about life which we use to make sense of
the world around us. While counsellors seek to be aware of their own
values and theories and not to impose them on other people, it is very
difficult to prevent this from ever happening. In addition, it is not
unusual for people who are learning how to cope better to use their
counsellor as a model, and to imitate the counsellor's actions, and to
take in certain of the counsellor's beliefs and attitudes as their own
(Munro *et al.*, 1983). Giving encouragement to move through the
stages to be described below can be regarded in itself as a form of
direction or guidance because the process pushes the attention of the

person seeking help towards a path leading towards increased self-autonomy.

Along this path it is possible to distinguish four stages. These are not fixed stages which are always followed, rather they are generalizations about broad divisions which can be distinguished in a complex process, in the same way as it is possible to make generalizations about life stages. The details of each individual's journey on the road to greater self-help are unique to that person. The stages overlap with one another, and the counselling process rarely falls into them neatly and tidily. There is likely to be movement backwards and forwards between them. Each stage is discussed below in general terms; Chapter 3 will take each stage in turn and look in more detail at strategies and tactics used to implement it.

The first stage is that of helping a person to explore their problem. The counsellor encourages that person to describe his/her practical difficulties and associated feelings and thoughts. This may be difficult for some people, especially if, for instance, they are not very articulate, or are emotionally distressed. Counsellors make a point of developing a wide range of strategies and tactics, both verbal and non-verbal, such as active listening, and different types of questioning, so that they can select from them those most appropriate in a given situation with a particular person. They may encourage a person in need to look at his/her problems from different points of view, possibly in ways not used before. This process of exploration benefits both the helper and the person being helped by focusing attention where it is most needed, and giving some sense of direction as regards the kind of difficulties which need to be tackled.

The second stage is the understanding of a problem. The person in need is encouraged to clarify and analyze the problem, and issues which may surround it. Such issues may have their sources in external events and/or in processes internal to the person seeking help. The aim is to help the person in need to understand better the way in which he/she is thinking and feeling about the problem, and how he/she is relating to the external environment. It is a way of helping another to become more self-aware of both the assumptions and attitudes which he/she is bringing to bear on a situation, and the strategies and tactics being used to cope with it. How a person copes today depends not only on present circumstances, but also on attitudes and skills which represent the summation of solutions to every earlier crisis (Brown and Pedder 1979). As all of us move through life we develop ways of coping without necessarily altogether realizing exactly what these are. It takes practice to learn to 'listen to oneself', to be aware of how we act and of the many different types of messages which we give to ourselves, and also to listen to and be more observant of those with whom we interact.

The third stage which can be distinguished in the counselling approach to helping is that of decision making, that is, the stage at which the person seeking help starts to decide what to do about the problem confronting him/her. The process of achieving better understanding which was described in stage 2 is usually a necessary preliminary to evaluating personal strengths and weaknesses, and deciding how to build on the former and remedy the latter if at all possible; also it is an essential preliminary to weighing up whether there is any action which might be taken to modify a situation. Possible alternative courses of action are identified, and their advantages and disadvantages considered as far as this is possible, before a decision is made. Perhaps the person seeking help may decide on some short-term goals before moving to long-term goals. As already noted, changing direction and putting oneself in a new relationship to oneself and to the world is often felt to be full of risk, and it may be necessary to go forward in small steps in order to gain confidence.

The fourth stage is that of putting decisions into action. A counsellor gives encouragement and support at this time, and helps the person in need to reflect on the steps he/she is taking, and on the results.

As suggested above, these stages are not always worked through systematically. For example, initial exploration may be followed by analysis and better understanding of part of a problem, but the person seeking help may then become aware of other aspects which remain unclear, and need to return to the exploration stage. Perhaps a decision is reached about how to start coping with a problem and then implemented, but if results are unsatisfactory then it may be necessary to re-analyze the situation and find another way of tackling it.

Not all people who seek help from a counsellor need to pass through all these stages. Perhaps one person having been helped to analyze a problem more clearly feels capable of carrying on without further assistance; another person may come seeking help having analyzed the problem but in need of assistance in exploring and weighing up possible alternative courses of action, and so on. The counsellor has to find out the stage which each person has reached, and the nature and extent of the help which is being sought. The counsellor also has to take into account any time constraints. If it is possible to meet the person seeking help only once, then it may be necessary to concentrate most of the attention on one or two stages and move as rapidly as possible through the others.

Strategies used in the counselling process have been described here in broad terms. Individual counsellors develop their own styles of helping. These are influenced by personal knowledge and experiences and skills, by preferences for working in particular ways with those whom they are helping, and by the assumptions they make about how people learn to cope better with problems in living. Some counsellors favour a particular style associated with a particular school of counselling; an increasing number like to draw on several schools and to use the combination of strategies which seems best for the person seeking help. Readers who are interested in different theoretical approaches to counselling can find those most often used described and discussed in books such as those by Nelson-Jones (1982), Proctor (1978), and Dryden (1984). Some of the detailed methods which a counsellor may use to help others are described in Chapter 3 of this book.

THE CLIMATE OF HELPING

It has been pointed out that there are risks associated with changing direction in life, with doing, thinking and feeling in different ways, and with relating differently to the environment. It has also been suggested that the process leading up to change in direction is not always straightforward or easy for the person seeking help. Such a person is more likely to be willing to undertake this work if he/she feels it is safe to do so. If that person feels confident in and trusts the helper, and in turn feels that the helper has regard for and respects him/her as a person, then it is likely that it will be easier to talk openly, to explore hopes and fears, and to expose needs and weaknesses as well as strengths. A counsellor seeks to establish and maintain a climate in which the person seeking help is as much at ease as possible. The counsellor seeks to do this by a careful selection of methods, and of strategies and tactics, in combination with qualities he/she possesses as a person.

There is considerable debate as to what these personal qualities are. It is generally agreed that one of them must be empathy, and indeed it is difficult to see how counselling can take place without it, so this will be considered first. Empathy has been defined as being able 'to sense the client's private world as if it were your own, without ever losing the "as if" quality' (Rogers 1961, p. 284). Each of us interprets the self and the reality around ourselves in our own individual way. If a counsellor is to help another person, it is necessary to view life through the eyes of that other person, to enter into that individual's understanding of reality, and to be able to use his/her frame of reference. The counsellor can then stand back and use the knowledge so gained to help the person in need to find better ways of coping. It seems likely that the ability to empathize is partly inborn; it is probably also learnt from early experiences of parents and others, and is later encouraged by training. It requires such skills, for example, as being able to listen actively, knowing how to check on meanings, being alert for verbal and non-verbal messages which appear to contradict one another, — perhaps, for instance, an assertion that a particular incident 'is of no importance', but said with a break in the voice and a vigour which suggests anger, and so on.

A counsellor is able not only to empathize but also to communicate that empathy to the person being helped, so that that person can know and feel that he/she is understood. This can be done using such tactics as, for example, summarizing and paraphrasing, and also non-verbally through facial expressions, such as a nod of the head, and so on. These help to demonstrate interest in, understanding of, and an openness of mind to, the messages being given.

There may be difficulties in seeking to share both the more superficial and deeper thoughts and feelings of another person if the 'as if' quality is lost, for the helper may become overwhelmed by the experiences of the other. It is possible, for example, for the difficulties of another person to trigger off in the helper reciprocal feelings associated with a personal experience in the past. A skilled helper is able to recognize such reactions, and for the time being put on one side personal thoughts and feelings which hinder concentration on those of the person who is seeking help.

Rogers (1957) claims that there are three qualities which it is essential for a counsellor to possess, namely, empathy, warmth and genuineness. Warmth is sometimes described as 'unconditional positive regard'. It involves the active non-judgmental acceptance of another as he or she is, whatever characteristics come to light. It involves respect for and valuing of that person as a unique individual who has the right to decide how to live his/her own life, and has the resources to do so, even if those are temporarily blocked or perhaps require extending. This does not mean that the counsellor necessarily agrees with everything the person in need thinks, feels or does, nor condones practices considered dangerous to the well-being of other individuals or of society at large, nor that the counsellor should never express differences in outlook. What it does mean is that communications from the counsellor should convey care, concern, warmth and respect; a non-judgmental stance should not come over as coldness and distancing. The degree of warmth a helper displays may vary according to the needs of the person seeking help; some are helped by a more intimate relationship, and some by a more matter-of-fact one (Inskipp and Johns 1984).

It is not easy to describe in a few words what is meant by warmth, and this applies also to the quality of genuiness. If helpers are genuine then they are communicating openly. They are not 'putting on an act', or pretending to have knowledge, skills or qualities which they do not really possess. Verbal and non-verbal communications match each other, and it is not necessary for listeners to decode messages which are being given (Nelson-Jones 1983). Such helpers can be assertive without being aggressive, they do not need to be defensive, and are capable of deep self-disclosure if this is appropriate in the interests of the person being helped. They are aware not only of those inner feelings and experiences which may hinder the helping process, but also of those which can be drawn on to help a person in distress. It may be helpful on occasion, for instance, to give an illustration from one's own personal life of experiencing a feeling similar to that being described in order to help another person to feel that he/she is not the only human being ever to suffer that particular difficulty, and that it is possible for another person to understand. Being open does not mean, however, that a counsellor must always express all thoughts and feelings which are present. What it does mean is that what is shared is done so with sincerity, and in the course of counselling it is shared in the service of the person being helped.

As has already been suggested, in many learning situations modelling takes place. If a helper is genuine, then this may assist the person in need to admit to him/herself thoughts and feelings hitherto unknown or denied, and to become more open and forthcoming with others. The more an individual can do this when with the counsellor, the more it increases the possibility that the counsellor may be able to assist in the most appropriate way that particular person at that particular stage in their life's journey.

Empathy, warmth and genuiness interact with each other. Rogers considered these qualities sufficient for a helping relationship. Many others, such as Carkhuff (1969) and Egan (1975) would add others, one of which is concreteness. It is a little difficult to know whether this is better described as a quality or a strategy. It means the ability to reformulate vague and imprecise thoughts and feelings into more specific statements. It is an important attribute of those who seek to help themselves more skilfully, and is a way of describing how stages one and two outlined in the previous section, that is, exploration and understanding, may be applied on a small scale to individual aspects of a problem. It is not easy for a person in need to think through difficulties expressed in vague terms, such as 'I feel depressed', or 'Everything is getting on top of me'. A counsellor can encourage more concrete thinking by, for example, the skilled use of questions to elicit what being depressed or feeling overwhelmed by everything means to that person in terms of his/her thoughts, feelings and actions in relation to a particular situation at a particular point in time.

In the previous-section it was stated that the counselling process could be subdivided into four sections to convey a sense of the direction in which a counsellor moves in the process of helping persons in need to become more skilful in helping themselves, but that these stages were not sharply separated from one another and did not necessarily occur in that order. In this section four of the qualities which it is important for a counsellor to possess have been subdivided but they are no more discrete than are the stages. They overlap and run into one another. For example, encouraging a person to express him/herself in more concrete terms can be done in such a way that it also expresses warmth and empathy. The overall aim of creating an appropriate climate is to provide, in the words of Heron (1978, p. 189) 'Safety, security and support, and deep unqualified affirmation of the warmth of a human being'.

COUNSELLING AS A DYNAMIC HELPING RELATIONSHIP

A counselling relationship is a working relationship into which both helper and person being helped must put considerable effort if it is to prove useful. Both together engage in the process of learning and understanding as they seek a way forward for the person in difficulties. The quality of this relationship may of itself be of considerable

therapeutic value to a person in need of help, especially if the difficulties of that person include relationships with other people (Munro
et al., 1983). In the process of working on problems with another
person in a climate of safety, it is possible for an individual to try out
new ways of relating to another person, for example, being more
assertive, and to build up greater confidence in and respect for
him/herself.

One factor which may influence a counselling relationship, particularly in the initial stages, is the cultural context in which it takes
place. While it is accepted that children and the elderly, the sick and
the handicapped are dependent on others, at least to some degree,
adults generally are expected to be self-sufficient. A sense of low self-
esteem stemming from the need to seek help from another person
may add to the difficulties experienced by some people who come to
a counsellor. Added to this is the fact that many counsellors are
invested with a degree of authority as a result of the position to which
they have been appointed, in a counselling centre, hospital, school,
and so on, and as a result they may be held in some awe. It is not
uncommon for people seeking help to expect to be dependent and to
be told what to do. Part of the process of learning how to take different directions is learning how to respond to resources and
information offered by 'experts' in a straightforward, non-deferential
way, and to appraise and evaluate this help for its appropriateness to
the self (Proctor 1978, p. 248). A counsellor has the somewhat para-
doxical task as a relationship develops of encouraging evaluation of
the assistance which he or she is offering.

One way of working towards this ability to evaluate assistance is by
use of the strategy known as immediacy, which is a further feature
identified by some writers, such as Carkhuff (1969), as essential to the
helping relationship. The helper invites the person in need to concentrate on feelings and thoughts about the present, not about events in
the past or anticipated happenings in the future which are often the
chief preoccupation of discussions. The person seeking help is
encouraged to disclose spontaneously attitudes towards the helping
relationship as it is taking place in the here and now (Murgatroyd
1985).

In the early stages of a helping relationship the counsellor is
normally the one who exercises the greater initiative and control
over the interactions which take place. It is usually the counsellor
who gives direction to the conversation by, for example, encouraging the person in need to describe, reflect, analyze, and so on. As a

relationship develops, however, the counsellor increasingly takes a back seat so that the person seeking help can exercise more initiative, perhaps, for example, by deciding which aspect of the problem in hand shall be the focus of attention at any one time, and by weighing it up and making decisions with little or no prompting from the counsellor. Another paradox of a counsellor's work is that he/she seeks to become redundant as the person in need becomes more autonomous, and one way of working towards this is through the relationship itself with the person in need.

Because the relationship between counsellor and person being helped is so important it is necessary for both sides to be clear about the nature of it. There has to be mutual appreciation of such matters as the ways in which they are going to work together, and the type of work which they are going to do, and over the question of confidentiality, so that neither side harbours unrealistic expectations of the other. One way of describing this is to say that a contract is agreed between both sides. Sometimes drawing up a contract is treated as a task in itself. Sometimes understanding of the terms of the contract grows as the relationship develops between counsellor and person being helped. If necessary, a contract which is proving to be unsatisfactory as a relationship develops can be renegotiated. There is further discussion on contracting in Chapter 3.

These brief comments on the development of the relationship between helper and person being helped describe a dimension of the counselling process which is perhaps, like the characteristic of non-directiveness, not always recognized as important by the non-counsellor. It is completely inappropriate for the process of skilful helping to be regarded simply as a matter of one person who has help passing it over to another who is in need of it, as if some sort of present were being handed over.

A skilled counsellor is something of a researcher, a decision maker and an administrator at one and the same time. As a researcher, a counsellor is constantly gathering information about the person being helped and his/her problems and attitudes to these problems, reflecting on it, clarifying it, checking it for accuracy, and comparing it with information already received. As a decision maker, a counsellor is deciding which methods and strategies are important at any one time and which tactics to adopt to put them into practice, such as when to encourage a person in need to start making decisions about future actions. As an administrator, a counsellor is co-ordinating all his/her activities and the feedback from the person being helped, and checking on the development of the helping process as a whole.

In a helping relationship a person who has help to offer has more power than the person who seeks help. As the latter becomes more critical of the help offered, and takes greater initiatives in the relationship, and plays a larger part in negotiating a contract, then the asymmetry in the power relationship is reduced. Nevertheless, it is the counsellor who essentially remains in control.

Power carries with it responsibilities. Counsellors are not responsible for the lives of those whom they seek to help, but they are responsible on the one hand for their own lives, and on the other for how they relate to those whom they seek to help, and for the standard of service which they offer in their counselling work. These two areas of responsibility are intimately interconnected with one another. Carkhuff and Berenson (1977, p. 236), for example, suggest 'helping is as effective as the helper is living effectively'. This is a topic often neglected in the literature, as Nelson-Jones (1984) has pointed out, and will be referred to again later in this chapter.

WORKING WITH GROUPS

The discussion on counselling in this chapter has concentrated on one to one situations, but counsellors also work with groups. For example, in some workplaces a group might meet informally during lunch breaks, and some counsellors organize workshops which last for perhaps an hour, half a day, or one or several days. All the headings used in this chapter would be equally relevant for a chapter on group work because the basic principles of counselling are relevant however many people are being helped. There are, however, several features peculiar to work with groups to which attention should be drawn.

Groups have a life of their own. When people meet together with some aims or ideals in common, and believe that in this way they will be able to satisfy needs or to obtain rewards, then the group is likely to develop its own norms, or ways of working, its own roles and statuses, and its own power and emotional relationships. Members interact with one another, and are interdependent in so far as they are affected by and respond to any event that affects any of the group's members (Jacques 1984). Complexities of structure, of patterns of communication, and of the nature of relationships tend to increase the larger the group.

During the life of a group it is possible to discern not only stages of development in individual members but also stages in the development of the group as a unit. One of the tasks of the counsellor is to facilitate group development from initial stages of confusion and milling around, through a time when members try out different ways of relating to and working with one another and jockey for power, on to a situation of group consolidation. This process is as unlikely to take place in a neat and tidy fashion as is the development of the individual outlined in this chapter, but generalizations about it are useful for indicating overall directions in which the development is likely to take place. Some people who have studied the paths of development of groups have suggested more detailed stages which can be discerned using such criteria as amount of interaction, nature of interaction at cognitive, affective, and behavioural levels, and group structure and solidarity (for example, see Rogers 1970; Heron 1977).

Factors which may affect group development include whether the group is closed or open, how membership is selected, and the frequency and duration of meetings. Physical settings are also important, for they can act as constraints on group size and on the nature of the strategies and tactics which can be used. For instance, small-group work is difficult in a confined space and when furniture cannot be moved around. The organizational setting in which the meeting takes place may also be important. For example, if a workshop is run in a works unit to help staff to cope with stress at work, the staff may then seek to change features of work experience which they find tend to engender stress. Sometimes counsellors may be asked to co-operate with senior members of an organization in defining staff needs and in planning changes to meet them. A counsellor who acts in this way as a consultant is providing an indirect service to people in need of help.

A group leader has concern for, and pays attention to, both the development of a group as a whole and also the development of individual members. This can be very demanding because different people bring to a group different needs and resources, and develop in different directions at varying rates. Because of the complexities of the task it is not unusual in a workshop for there to be co-leaders, particularly if the group is large, and/or the topic at the centre of attention is emotionally charged — for example, ways of coping with bereavement.

It is important to recognize that group members are not dependent only on the leader for help, but can help one another. They can exchange information, explore with one another new strategies and tactics, give each other emotional support, and so on. This is particularly important when interpersonal relationships are a significant issue in the group's overall aim. One of the leader's tasks is to encourage the development of a group's potential. This can be done by using a variety of learning activities which give members opportunities to interact with one another in different ways, in role play or small group tasks, for instance, and also by seeking to develop a climate in which individuals feel it is safe to work both with one another and with the leader.

It is as important to have a contract in a group situation as it is in one to one interaction. Members need to know what they can expect not only of the leader but also of one another. In a group there is potential for much co-operation, but there is also potential for much confusion, conflict and frustration if expectations are at variance. Group contracts are likely to include agreement on a variety of points about inter-relationships and responsibility, for example, that each person shall talk for himself or herself and not for anyone else; that each person shall be responsible for his/her own behaviour; that people shall accept, and not judge, each other's feelings; and that they shall talk *to* other people, not *about* them. A book written by members of the Coping with Crisis Research Group (1986) describes how six different types of workshops were organized and run, and factors which influenced them, and illustrates a number of the points referred to in this section.

RESPONSIBILITIES IN COUNSELLING

There is a tendency to look up to 'experts' as people who must know all the answers, and perhaps a temptation on the part of the experts to act the part! Some people hold a mythical picture of a counsellor as someone who loves all people, has a well-ordered personal life, and is always fair and impartial. Counsellors are human beings, and, like all human beings, they have their own problems in living. They have been or are involved at first hand in situations which involve pain, and have had to look for ways in which it may be faced. This can be a strength if they are able to use in the service of others knowledge gained from experience. Counselling involves combining the knowledge and skills gained from personal practical experience, from studying the helping process in theoretical terms, from trying it out in the safety of experimental situations, and from practising the process as a professional. A skilled helper knows that there is always more to find out about the helping process and accepts responsibility for his/her own continuing professional development. This necessitates being someone who continues to learn, constantly on the look-out for ways and means of increasing resources and improving the quality of the help offered.

Making a judgment about whether the help being offered is the most appropriate for a particular person in a particular situation is not easy. No person can ever enter fully into the reality of another, however skilful the strategies used or however favourable the climate. Each of us has a part of ourselves which we keep hidden from the view of others. We each have our secrets, and these are indispensable to us because they enable us to retain an enduring sense of identity; the secrets belong to us, and to us alone (Bok 1982). To some extent we can each decide how much of ourselves to reveal to or keep from another person, but we may give off messages about ourselves and our underlying outlook on life which we do not intend to convey. In everyday life we try to present ourselves as we want others to see us, but may not always fully succeed (Goffman 1969). A counsellor is aware that there may be discrepancies between what is 'given' and what is 'given off', and can use information so gathered constructively in the helping process. But in this two-way process the same principles apply to the counsellor, who also 'gives' and 'gives off' messages. It can be expressed as a diagram, known as the 'Johari window', named after the originators *Jo*e Luft and *Har*ry *In*gham (1955).

	Known to self	Unknown to self
Known to others	Free and open: You know and others know.	Blind self: You don't know but others do.
Unknown to others	Hidden self: You know but others do not.	Unknown self: You don't know and others don't know.

Figure 2.1   *The 'Johari window'*

Counsellors must, therefore, tolerate uncertainty about the appropriateness of the help which they are giving and the difficulties inherent in the process of relating to another human being. They also have to recognize that whatever help is offered may be rejected or may be interpreted in ways other than those intended. In addition, because counselling is orientated towards helping in the long term, a counsellor may never know how useful is the work he/she puts into helping someone in need. For the skilled helper uncertainty is a challenge to carry on learning and to provide the best service possible, not an excuse to shrug the shoulders and rest on his/her laurels.

To accept the challenge requires strong motivation. A counsellor needs to be honest with him/herself about the reasons for doing this particular type of work. It can be argued that there is no such quality as pure altruism. People's motives for helping others are normally mixed. It is somewhat difficult to understand how counsellors can continue to be skilled helpers and on-going learners without a sincere wish to assist others in a constructive way. Other elements which may enter the desire to counsel, however, may include: helping others in order to avoid dealing with personal problems, perhaps, for example, seeking to get close to others in more formal situations because of being unable to achieve closeness in informal personal relationships; seeking reward from experiencing a sense of status and power in the helping relationship; if the job carries remuneration, regarding it in instrumental terms. A counsellor has a responsibility to be aware of and to understand his or her personal motivations in order to avoid letting them get in the way of the process of helping others constructively.

Because the helping process is so complex, it is not always easy to sort out the respective responsibilities of helper and helped in the relationship which they have with one another. It is possible for a counsellor to err, however unintentionally, on the side of accepting too much responsibility, thereby hindering the person seeking help from becoming more autonomous even when that person may be ready to be so. It is also possible for a counsellor to accept too little responsibility, perhaps by not monitoring carefully enough the development of the helping relationship and encouraging a person in need to make decisions before that person has sufficient understanding and resources to do so. If there are difficulties, a counsellor must be able to practise skills he/she encourages in persons seeking help, that is, to stand back, analyze a situation and factors impinging on it, weigh up different courses of action, and make a decision on how to proceed. For example, if a person in need appears to be making little progress, a counsellor has a responsibility to consider the reason. Perhaps the help being offered is inappropriate and requires some initiative on the counsellor's part, for example, trying alternative approaches, or suggesting that the person in need should be referred to someone else who has a different range of resources; or perhaps the person and his/her problems is triggering off in the counsellor thoughts and feelings which are getting in the way of the helping process, and which the counsellor needs to sort out. On the other hand, perhaps the person seeking help appears to be reluctant to make much effort to use help being offered, and in this case the counsellor might, for example, decide to confront the person tactfully and diplomatically with the situation and talk it through. Perhaps a combination of factors such as these is influencing the situation.

Reference was made in a previous section to the suggestion that there is a close connection between how counsellors live their own lives and the standard of-service offered. Counsellors encourage others to develop a variety of skills and qualities, but cannot expect more from others than they are capable of themselves. Responsibility for helping the self is interlinked with the responsibility associated with helping others.

This applies to general preparedness for the task of helping as well as to specific skills and qualities. Counselling is hard work. It is associated with uncertainties, it requires intense concentration, and it can leave the practitioner feeling drained and exhausted. Counsellors need resources outside themselves on which they can draw both to gain help, if necessary, with personal difficulties inside and outside the counselling relationship, and also to provide means of relaxation and general renewal of well-being. Other people, such as fellow counsellors, counselling consultants, family, and friends can all play a part, as can books, courses, and so on. It is important when much working time is spent serving others to have pursuits which contribute towards personal fulfilment, for example, some hobbies. How the helper is helped is an important consideration.

Counsellors cannot equip themselves with resources and claim that they have no deficits. Similarly they can help persons in need to improve their resources but not to become çompletely equipped to cope with their difficulties; the concept of cure is inappropriate in counselling. There is always scope for both helpers and those whom they help to increase resources relative to deficits, but standing still,

or even backsliding is always possible. 'Personal responsibility is a
continuous struggle between resources and defects within each and
across all psychological skills' (Nelson-Jones 1984, p. 97). The personal responsibility of counsellors encompasses both their own lives
and their counselling interviews.

CONCLUDING COMMENTS

The aim of this chapter has been to look at some of the fundamental
principles and skills on which the process of counselling is based, in
the belief that a study of them can benefit people who, whether formally or informally, seek to help others. It is not possible to formulate
a neat and tidy rulebook of 'do's and 'don't's' with regard to the
helping process because it is so complex. What has been done is to
direct attention to a number of important aspects of it, and to give
some indication of the guidelines with which counsellors work,
because these guidelines are relevant to many forms of helping
which take place between adults.

It was suggested in the course of the discussion in this chapter that
there are two features of the counselling process as a whole of which
many non-counsellors may not be fully aware. The first is its non-
directiveness, and the second is that the nature of the working relationship between helper and person being helped is normally of itself
an important ingredient in the helping process. These two features
are closely interlinked. In order to find a way forward both the helper
and the person being helped must work together in partnership. It is
not appropriate to view the helping process in terms of a helper
bringing along a pre-packaged bundle of help which is passed over to
a passive receiver. Each person in need is travelling on his/her own
unique journey through a time of change. The helper needs to have a
range of resources and, as the relationship develops and more is
learnt about the person in need and the nature of the needs and the
way in which the person is coping, the helper draws on those
resources as seems most appropriate. The person in need has the
opportunity to learn how to make use of those resources, which
include the relationship itself, to increase his/her ability to cope in
ways more personally satisfactorily with difficulties encountered on
the journey through change.

There are many different questions which helpers might ask themselves about how they might improve their ability to play their part in

the helping process as constructively as possible. There are questions about the person seeking help. For example, how clear an understanding does that person have of his/her problems? Is that person ready to move forward, or is it better to pause before giving opportunities designed to encourage the search towards greater self-help? How much motivation does that person have to move forward? Does that person need to learn more about particular skills, say, increasing self-awareness?

There are questions a helper can ask of him/herself. For example, do I need to concentrate on becoming more self-aware of my own values and assumptions so as not to run the risk of imposing them on others? Am I too anxious to see instant positive results, and to receive thanks for my efforts at helping, and am I prepared to accept that my efforts may be rejected? Do I need to increase my range of strategies and tactics so that I am better able to gather information, and do I check carefully enough on my understanding of another person's problems? Do I convey effectively enough my empathy, warmth and genuiness? Do I perhaps need to pay more attention to cultivating these qualities in myself, and also other abilities such as concreteness and immediacy? Do I have sources of outside help and ways of renewing myself as a person?

There are questions a helper can ask about the development of the helping relationship. For example, do I keep track carefully enough of where it has come from, and where it is now, and the direction in which it is moving? Do I sufficiently often review the responsibilities which I and the person I am helping are shouldering in this relationship?

The process of helping is open-ended; it can never be perfected. There are always questions to keep on asking. By its very nature it is a source of stimulation and challenge to those who wish to learn more about it. And by improving our way of tackling it we are in a better position to help others to make the most of whatever opportunities they may have to improve the quality of their lives.

CHAPTER THREE

Counselling in
Action

INTRODUCTION

The previous chapter outlined the basic nature of counselling and
guidance work in adult and continuing education. It gave emphasis to
the idea that helping is a dynamic process in which the person in need
is encouraged to explore their presenting problem, enabled to understand that problem and its meaning for them, helped to make a decision and supported when they acted on that decision. Whilst helping
can be pursued by means of a variety of strategies and tactics (and
conceptualized through a variety of models), it invariably involves
the helper in attending to the verbal and non-verbal behaviour of the
person, assessing, advising, teaching, coaching, evaluating and providing feedback (Miller 1982).

In order to perform such a helping role, helpers need to communicate to those in need empathy, warmth and genuineness, and show
that they are 'sticking close to the knitting' of the problem that they
are presenting (Rogers 1961). Sometimes they may need to challenge
the assumption the person is making about their situation: confrontation is therefore another part of the helper's repertoire. But the
framework of helping requires the development of trust and
mutuality as well as progress towards some action which directly
helps the person in need.

Different needs and different people require helpers to adopt
different strategies and tactics when helping them. The person seeking help with anxiety about examinations may need a different
helping approach from the person seeking help because of difficulties
in their relationships with another adult or group of adults. Helpers
therefore need to possess a range of skills appropriate to the

situations which those who typically seek their help present. In addition, helpers need to recognize their own limits (Murgatroyd 1985) so as to provide a basis for referring people to appropriate helping agencies in the community, and so as to avoid becoming a part of the problem for the person in need. Some of these limits to helping concern the skills and abilities of the helper, others the practical resources (time and space) and organizational constraints within which they work. The helpers can help themselves, as the previous chapter indicated, by having clear contracts for helping with those with whom they are working.

In this chapter we elaborate on these ideas and describe some of the detailed methods by which one person can help others. In doing so we offer descriptions which are intended to be appropriate to a variety of individuals working with adults in a variety of settings. These include: adult education centres and extra-mural departments, institutions of further and higher education, government training and community development schemes, the workplace, voluntary organizations and other agencies. In addition, we present short case studies of the ways in which individuals can be helped with two specific problems — examination anxiety, and feeling put down by others — so that the way in which the skills described here are used in practice can be clearly seen.

A single chapter in a book cannot describe in detail the strategies and tactics of helping. Others offer detailed suggestions for helping — we recommend Eisenberg and Delaney (1977), Munro *et al.* (1983), Murgatroyd (1985) and Nelson-Jones (1983) as excellent books for the further exploration of the skills described here. One thing that must be emphasized at the outset and re-emphasized throughout is the fundamental nature of the processes we describe here. They are not a set of mechanical tools for helpers to apply. Rather, they are powerful skills which, when used sensitively and with care, are likely to encourage the person in need to reach their own understanding of their situation and thus enable them to make their own decisions and take an action or set of actions appropriate to their needs. When used insensitively or without care, these same skills can make the life of the person in need more difficult. They are presented here in the context of the model of helping established in the previous chapter. This model involved four stages of work — exploration, understanding, decision making and action. These too are not mechanical stages that the helper works through systematically. Each time, the helper will find that the tasks associated with these stages run into each other, that they sometimes embark upon something that leads to a dead-end, that there are false starts and hopes. By examining each of the four stages in turn and in detail here, we do not wish to suggest that this is the pattern of helping that is most common in adult education. Rather, we are using these stages as a device for introducing some ideas about helping. At all stages of the helping process, the helper needs to communicate to the person in need empathy, warmth and genuineness. In addition, they need to focus upon the concrete issues which that person wishes to discuss, and upon building a sound working relationship. The stages outlined here are meaningless unless these basic conditions for an effective helping relationship are met.

One final introductory point. When someone finds that they are acting as a helper to another person, even though this is not their normal role and they feel that they have had little training for the role in which they now find themselves, there is a need to remember that the professionalization of helping is a relatively recent phenomenon (Wilding 1982). Helping is a natural and essentially human process: your own frailty as a helper is precisely the human quality that the person in need is calling on at the time of their need. Whilst we do not suggest that you engage in helping when you feel that the task is beyond you, we do suggest that feelings of uncertainty about the helping process are held by almost all professionals. As long as this feeling encourages learning by the helper and the helping relationship is one of mutual learning and development, it can be regarded as healthy.

EXPLORATION

To help the person understand their situation and the problem that they present, it is first necessary to help them to explore this problem. How this is done will depend upon the problem itself. But there are some basic helping skills that are useful in the exploratory phase of helping.

The most critical skill is creative listening (Pinney 1981) or active listening (Nelson-Jones 1983). The helper seeks to attend totally to the statements the person in need makes and does so with the intention of not only fully understanding these statements but also understanding how this person must feel and think about the situations they describe. That is, the helper seeks to use listening as a basis for the development of accurate empathy. The helper needs to listen to more than the words used in order to achieve such empathy. They need also to attend to the nature of that talk — its volume, how particular words are stressed and emphasized, the clarity with which the person is able to describe their situation and their experiences, the pace of the statements the person makes and the use the person makes of silences. They also need to look at the non-verbal behaviour of the person — does it match the statements (is it congruent), does their posture look tense or relaxed, are their facial expressions in tune with the statements, are they making eye contact with you or avoiding it and how is this to be interpreted? All of these attending behaviours are critical to the success of this exploratory phase. They enable the helper to 'get inside' the world of the person in need in a direct and illuminative way. Just listening and attending in these ways is often a form of helping.

But listening and attending is not enough to persuade the person in need that you are helping. The listening and attending needs to be active listening. This means that the helper needs to *communicate* that they are listening and attending without dominating the session. This can be done in a variety of ways. The first is to provide reflection of content — recap in a condensed summary what the person has just said in terms of what has happened to them. If someone is describing an accident and is going into details, occasionally summarizing the 'story so far' — this is reflection of content. The second is to provide reflection of feelings — to go behind the words used and summarize the way the person feels. In the example of the accident, a statement like '. . . as a result of these events you feel unsafe and insecure, not sure when you will be able to face others again, is that right?' — is a way of reflecting feelings back to the person whilst letting them maintain the initiative in talking.

Both of these kinds of reflection are facilitated by the helper being in a physical position conducive to helping. It is helpful to sit about 5 feet apart at the same level but at a slight angle and appearing moderately relaxed (Nelson-Jones 1983). The aim of the helper should be to give attention in an atmosphere of care and concern.

Reflection of feeling and content are starting points to the process of exploration. The helper can encourage the person in need to develop their exploration by using open questions (questions which have a variety of possible answers depending upon the way in which the person in need understands their situation) rather than closed questions (questions requiring either a 'yes' or 'no' response). They can also encourage talk by the use of minimal encouragers — little phrases that encourage talk ('Tell me more . . .', 'Uhm, uhm', 'Can you take that idea further . . .'), or by the use of transitional summaries in which the helper encourages the person to move to another feature of their situation (e.g. 'So far you've told me . . . now can you tell me how this connects to . . .').

Whilst these skills help the person to explore their presenting problem in their own terms, it is also necessary for the helper to avoid certain behaviours. These include: (a) directing and instructing — telling the person in need what they can or cannot talk about or re-interpreting what they do talk about in terms which the person in need does not recognize; (b) judging and evaluating — acting like a judge and jury about what the person should or should not have done and making it clear that the help being offered is conditional on the person accepting these judgments; (c) patronizing, moralizing, preaching and canvassing — telling the person in need what they ought or ought not do, including comments based on 'If I were you . . .'; (d) labelling and diagnosing — putting the person in need into some box or category (another middle-aged woman, a lazy student, a depressive) and then working with that category or box rather than the person in need; (e) offering false reassurances ('Oh I am sure everything will turn out fine, just you see . . .') in the absence of evidence; (f) interrogating — making questions sound as if the person in need is guilty of something or is in trouble and you are going to 'get to the bottom of it'; (g) over-interpreting and making a psychological problem out of nothing — offering explanations of the way the person feels or behaved which bear little relationship to their situation or experience; (h) inappropriately self-disclosing — talking about self in ways and at times when it is not appropriate to do so; and (i) what we like to call 'being too clever by half' — offering instant solutions to the problems the person in need presents which involve too many risks for that person to take. It is as important to avoid these common mistakes in helping as it is to work at the skills just outlined.

It is also important, during this exploratory period of a helping relationship, to offer encouragement to the person in need not only to talk but also to use their own latent abilities to cope. This is necessary, since for many people seeking the help of an adult educator or a guidance worker in a voluntary organization there is a very limited time in which help can be given (mainly because helping sessions are short and infrequent, and the helping process is generally over a short period of time). There are three specific ways of helping persons gain self-esteem through exploration. The first is to offer contingent praise (Janis 1982) — offering praise for specific accomplishments, actions or intentions which are in line with the needs the person in need is expressing. The second is to offer non-contingent acceptance — statements that show that the helper is accepted as a worthwhile person and is held in high regard, despite whatever shortcomings and weaknesses they elaborate (Goldstein 1975; Rogers and Dymond 1954). Finally, the helper can encourage the person to enrich their self-esteem by building their confidence in their ability to analyze and interpret their own problems from their point of view (Janis 1982). In using these (and other) skills the helper is seeking to think with rather than for the person in need (Brammer and Shostrom 1968).

At the end of this phase of helping, the helper and the person in need will need to: (a) have a clear understanding of the problem faced by the person in need from that person's point of view; (b) have a sense of the kinds of outcomes they desire from the helping process; and (c) have a contract for working together.

This idea of a working contract needs some elaboration, since many will be unfamiliar with the assumptions that it involves. Because a helper's time and resources are limited and because helping, to be effective, needs to be directed towards some purpose, a contract establishes the framework for helping an individual. The contract itself may be orally agreed or written (the latter is rare in Britain). Murgatroyd (1985) suggests that contracts need to deal with some or all of the following issues:

- How long the helping relationship will last (days, weeks, months)?
- How long and how frequent will a helping session be (once, twice or three times a week, for 15, 30 or 60 minutes)?
- Is the person in need expected to undertake any tasks in between helping sessions?
- What expectations should the person in need have about the sessions themselves — will they always be 'talking-sessions' or might other helping tactics be used?
- What is the position with regard to confidentiality?
- What are the specific goals of this helping work — can you agree on these goals before you start to move from the exploration stage to the understanding and deciding stages?

- Under what conditions can the helping work be terminated and by whom?
- Under what conditions can the person in need contact the helper outside the agreed sessions times (if at all)?

There may be other elements in the contract, but these are the basic features of most contracts. The reason they are helpful is that they make clear just what is expected of each party in the helping relationship. In addition, they ensure that helping is a structured and deliberate process on the part of both the helper and the person in need. This is essential if helping is to be more than an occasional chat or a series of haphazard encounters.

The offering of such a contract is also an important symbolic step in a helping relationship. It provides the helper with an opportunity to further enhance the self-esteem of the person in need and to give encouragement to that person to carry on their own attempts to help themselves, in parallel with the helping relationship they are developing.

All of the skills mentioned in this section are relevant to helpers of any kind who work with adults. They are not especially technical or difficult skills to develop, though all require practice and attention. What is important is that the skills are used in the context of building a relationship based on empathy, warmth, genuineness and concreteness (see Chapter 2).

UNDERSTANDING

The second stage of the helping process as described in the previous chapter concerns understanding. This involves the helper understanding the way in which the presenting problem the person in need has outlined tells us something about that person, and working with the person in need so that he or she achieves that understanding. In this section of the chapter this phase of work is explored by examining three areas of understanding: thinking, feeling and social relationships. This approach is taken so as to illuminate the way in which a variety of helping skills can be used to promote understanding and insight on the part of the person in need.

Thinking

A starting point for helping the person in need to look at their understanding of their own situation and the meaning it carries for them is to encourage them to look at the way they are thinking. That is, to help to identify not what they are thinking (the specific thoughts) but how they are thinking (the pattern of their thoughts). Often, the thinking strategy the person is using is a source of distress or self-doubt. For example, the student who thinks that they stand 'no chance' of passing an examination because they have failed to pass a previous examination is, by thinking in this way, making it difficult for others to help them or for them to help themselves. A person who is upset by the fact that others do not count them in their clique and feels that this means that no one likes them is distressed not by the actions of others but by the thoughts that they themselves harbour about their 'self'. The helper needs to encourage the person to look behind their immediate thoughts to the way in which these thoughts form a pattern for their thinking.

There are some common thinking problems which people in need display when seeking help. The first is projection — others are blamed for the way that they think and feel. The person makes statements like 'It's all her fault that I feel like this. . . .' or 'If it'd been clearer what this course was about then I wouldn't. . . .', or 'Until he said that about me I could cope, now I am not so sure . . .'. Blaming others for how one feels means that one is seeking to avoid responsibility for the way in which one feels. Whilst others may contribute to the way a feeling emerges, that feeling comes from within the self of the person in need. The opposite of projection is introjection in which the person takes it upon themselves to worry and experience distress on behalf of others. The person is denying their own thoughts and feelings so as to take on board the thoughts and feelings of others. Doing so helps them control their relationships with others whilst at the same time enabling them to deny their own feelings. This can take the many forms, including 'I am very worried about others in this class who I don't think are coping. . . .' and 'I just get very anxious when I think of all those people being asked to do this . . .'. What is implicit is that they are also anxious or worried for themselves, but they wish to deny this. Why it is worth looking for and helping the person to identify if it is present as a thinking strategy is that a great deal of the distress it causes is unnecessary. A third thinking strategy is called denial — the person's stress comes from their refusal to face up to the reality of their situation. A related thinking strategy here is wishful thinking in which the person both denies the reality of their situation whilst at the same time harbouring a fantasy about a favourable outcome — 'I haven't done any work for this exam, in fact for the course . . . but I am pretty good in exams and I haven't failed one yet! But I would like you to help me make sure . . .'. All of these represent particular thinking processes which might lie behind the person's reason for help seeking.

Albert Ellis (1962) has outlined a series of ideas about the way in which thinking patterns can create distress, and these ideas have been elaborated and developed by Dryden (1984). They suggest that a person in distress is distressed not by some activating event (A) but by their beliefs about this event (B) — it is the irrational beliefs an individual holds that has the consequence (C) of making the person feel stressed, unhappy, concerned, distressed, anxious, depressed or whatever. The activating events that Ellis looks at are many and varied — they can be external events (requirements set by others), or particular compulsions the person themselves feel to be important (what might be termed internal events). An example of an external event is the requirement to make a particular choice of a new course of study on a particular day; an equivalent internal event would be a desire to make a course choice that a particular parent would be pleased with. What matters is not the event, but the way that event is experienced in thought by the person in need. If the event is handled rationally in thought then it should not produce distress; where distress occurs it is largely due to 'faulty' or irrational thinking.

To help understand this idea, Ellis (1962) offers a list of irrational beliefs which he claims are common amongst those who seek help with stress, anxiety, depression or self-doubt. The beliefs listed below are irrational because: (a) they lead to distress and other negative emotions; (b) they are too absolute and contain 'must', 'should', 'ought-to' and 'have-to' statements which encourage the person to see desires as demands; and (c) the desires which these irrational thoughts contain are quickly escalated into demands which cannot be met thus guaranteeing failure for the person. The experience of holding irrational beliefs encourages the person to do two things: (a) 'musturbate' — to escalate desires into demands; and (b) 'awfulise — to experience the failure to meet demands as terrible, awful and ghastly rather than as unfortunate or just one of those things. The common irrational beliefs are, according to Ellis (1962) and as described by Murgatroyd (1985):

1) 'It is a dire necessity that I be loved or approved of by everyone for everything I do.'

2 'Certain acts are wrong and evil and those who perform these acts should be severely punished.'
3 'It is terrible, awful, horrible and catastrophic when things are not as I would like them to be.'
4 'Unhappiness is caused by external events, other people and circumstances and there is absolutely nothing I can do about it.'
5 'If something is or may be dangerous, fearsome or involves a risk I should be terribly worried about it and this worry should be my dominant thought.'
6 'It is easier to avoid or replace life's difficulties rather than to face up to them.'
7 'I need something or someone stronger or greater than myself upon which or whom I can rely.'
8 'I should be thoroughly competent, adequate and achieving at all times and in all the things I do and I should be recognized for the skills I have by all who know and work with me.'
9 'Because something in my past strongly affected my life, it should and will always affect me.'
10 'What others do is vitally important to my existence and I should therefore make great efforts to change them to be more like the people I would like them to be.'
11 'Human happiness can be achieved by inertia and inaction — if I wait here long enough it must come to me.'
12 'I have virtually no control over my emotions and I just cannot help feeling certain things.'

This is not an exhaustive list of irrational beliefs, but a list of the most common. What Ellis, Dryden and others suggest is that the elevation of these thoughts into dominant features of a person's thinking is likely to be the major source of distress for that person. The task of the helper is to help the person in need recognize which of these thoughts they seem to be using and help them see ways in which the use of these thoughts can contribute to or cause their distress. In pursuing this task the helper is seeking to encourage the person in need to realize for themselves how their thinking patterns affect their feelings and behaviour — they are still facilitating self-understanding rather than telling the person in need what it is that they see and hear.

One final point in relation to this work. Victor Frankl (1969) observes that many of those who seek help engage in what he calls 'hyper-reflection' — the person excessively dwells upon their inner thoughts and feelings to the point at which they are incapable of changing them because they have become so attached to them. He suggests that a significant role for a helper is to encourage de-reflection — discouraging the person from spending time thinking about their situation and encouraging them to act. This is an important observation: many adult learners who report being 'stuck' with the mastery of some concept or skill not only hold the irrational belief that they should be thoroughly competent and achieving at all times (belief 8 above) but also they spend a large amount of their time worrying about it. Indeed, they worry about not worrying enough and become anxious about being anxious.

Feelings

In seeking to help the person in need understand their feelings and the way in which their feelings have an impact on their thoughts and behaviour, the helper has the task of enabling the person to better discriminate between the different feelings they experience and to encourage the person to accept responsibility for the feelings that they have.

The notion of 'accepting responsibility' for feelings needs some explanation. When a person is depressed because something has happened to them (e.g. they have failed an important examination, have ended a relationship, cannot seem to master difficult ideas) it is important to recognize that the depression is something that is their response to their understanding of their situation. The feeling is not imposed by the situation, it is their response to it. Whilst many others will respond in just the same way, there is a uniqueness in the response which makes it 'their own'. By realizing that this is the case, the person in need can be helped to find ways of changing their responses so as to change the way they feel about the situation.

A first step is to encourage the person to discriminate accurately between different kinds of feelings. For example, when a person is angry they are often also anxious. A helper who seeks to encourage the person to understand accurately all of the feelings that they have will be in a stronger position to help that person. Another common feature of helping is that the person in need 'globalizes' their feelings — they so over-generalize their statements about the way that they feel that they make changing the way they feel more difficult. For example, just saying that they feel 'depressed' tells us little about what it is that they are feeling. The helper needs to get behind this label and find out precisely what they mean by feeling depressed — are they lethargic, bored, anxious, uncertain, weak, etc.? The helper's task is to enable the person to 'fine tune' their feelings so that they themselves better understand them.

Some useful techniques for helping the person in need to understand their feelings are given in James and Savary (1977) and in Murgatroyd (1985). In addition, the works of Eric Berne (1964; 1972) in describing transactional analysis and its applications are helpful.

A useful technique that helpers can use, whatever their role within an organization or the community, concerns the language employed by the person in need. For example, help seekers often speak of a particular feeling that they are experiencing as 'it' — 'it just comes over me . . .' or 'I can feel it rising up inside me . . .'. The use of 'it' in this way helps the person maintain a view of their feelings as something apart from themselves. To help the person better understand their feelings, encourage them to use 'I' instead of 'it' — this encourages ownership of feeling and requires the person to think more carefully about what happens within them when their feelings affect them. A related language device is to discourage the use of 'can't' (as in 'I just can't stop feeling like this . . .') and ask the person to use 'won't' instead ('I won't stop feeling like this . . .). Again, this device is intended to enable the person to own their feelings and their consequences. Finally here, the helper should discourage the person from asking 'why' questions about their feelings (e.g. 'Why do I feel . . .'): ask them to convert these questions into statements that they can make about their feelings.

These language devices are just some of the tactics available to the helper who wishes to encourage the person in need to explore the way that they feel. There are more powerful tactics available. These include the use of dreams, images, art therapy, role play, drama therapy and dance therapy methods, and many other devices (see Murgatroyd 1985). One particular technique which is both powerful and relatively easy to use involves the use of empty chairs. Imagine a person who is feeling uncertain and unhappy about a decision that they have to make (say, a decision about whether to accept the offer of a job or to stay on in education). There are many sides to this decision and many arguments for and against. These arguments are usually rehearsed passively in the mind of the person in need. Rather than simply sit and listen to these arguments for and against, the helper asks the person in need to sit in chair no. 1 when they wish to argue in favour of accepting the job and in chair no. 2 when they wish to argue in favour of continuing their education. The helper encourages the argument to be as confronting as possible, always ensuring that the correct chair is being occupied when the argument is being advanced. If other options emerge (like taking the job but ensuring day release) then an additional chair is added for each argument. The physical movement and the requirement to argue strongly from the position required by the occupancy of a particular chair sharpens the perception of the problem and increases both the helper's and the person in need's understanding of the feelings underlying the arguments used. This is a powerful and active device which has been used successfully on many occasions when just talking appeared to result in the person seeking help becoming 'stuck'. It works well with other problems — about marriage (a chair for the other partner's point of view), work (a chair for each person affected by the work problem) or in terms of understanding some conceptual problem (a chair for each view of the concept). The helper can use these devices — and many more like them — to help the person better understand just how they feel.

Social relationships

Several kinds of problems which helpers are asked to help with concern the ability of the person in need to relate to others socially, especially in groups. An important task for the helper is to encourage the person in need to fully understand the nature of their social difficulties, if these are present.

One area of concern for many is their level of social skills. Individuals feel inadequate at relating to others in groups, especially small groups in which they are expected to speak or work with others. They may also feel uncertain about forging a relationship with another person — be it a loving relationship or a work relationship. They need help in understanding what it is about their skills that is in need of attention and what behaviours they currently engage in that make their lack of social skills an impairment to relationships.

The helper can do much to assist the person in identifying their current level of skill, both through discussion and the use of role play (the latter being especially appropriate if the helper is working in a group context). Works by Trower *et al.* (1978), Falloon *et al.* (1974) and Liberman (1975) all provide useful source materials for the helper. Murgatroyd (1985), in a basic outline of this area of work, suggests that the helper needs to discern the extent to which some or all of the following social skill areas cause the person in need social difficulty: (a) observation skills — their ability to accurately understand the situation in which they find themselves; (b) listening skills — the extent to which the person in need is able to listen and understand what they hear and to appreciate the implications of what they hear; (c) speaking skills — the clarity with which a person is able to describe accurately their thoughts, feelings and experiences; (d) 'meshing' skills — the ease with which the person in need is able to relate to others without seeking to dominate; (e) expression of attitudes — how to express the attitudes and beliefs held without being aggressive; and (f) social routines — the ability to greet, make requests, gain access, talk to strangers, give and show sympathy, provide explanations, save face, offer apologies and say farewell with dignity and in a self-assured way. Establishing just how these skills are used and how their absence contributes to the problem which the person in need presents is a key to accurate understanding of this feature of the person.

Common to the problems presented under this heading to helpers (especially from women returning to learning and men who have experienced long-term unemployment) is an absence of assertiveness. Assertiveness is defined as the non-aggressive statement of a need in a way that shows respect and understanding for the needs of others. Individuals who feel rejected or dejected at the quality of their social relationships are often un-assertive or overly aggressive. This appears in situations when the person feels inhibited in the presence of others or feels manipulated or frustrated or lacking in confidence. It is perhaps most clearly seen when the person feels unable to say 'no' to a suggestion or a request because to do so would leave them feeling guilty. The helper's task is to examine the extent to which the person in need is lacking in assertiveness and to examine the strategies and tactics which the person uses to maintain their un-assertiveness. The text by Lange and Jakubowski (1978) provides helpful guides for the helper and suggestions for training activities.

In pursuing this task of understanding, the helper needs to continue to work with rather than for the person in need, and needs to undertake the task in the context of a clear contract and in the framework of an empathetic, warm and genuine helping relationship that 'sticks to the knitting' of the problem presented. The task is to understand the person and their experience of some given situation, and to do so in such a way as to suggest some possible actions and decisions for the person in need to take.

DECISION MAKING

The third stage of the helping process involves helping the person in need come to a decision about what it is they might do or how they wish to be. Whereas the previous activities have involved clarifying and understanding, the helper is now seeking to encourage the person to act in a more direct and positive way. Notice that we say 'encourages the person' and not 'instructs the person' or 'tells the person'. Our view of the helping process is that it is most effective when the person in need feels that they control the outcomes of helping. The task for the helper is to enable the person in need to make a clear decision about what they should do and how they should be.

Another way of expressing this is that the helper should enable the person in need to set themselves realistic goals for action — goals which they can reasonably expect to accomplish and which will have an impact on the problem they are presenting.

Some valuable pointers concerning how this can be achieved are given by Janis and Mann (1982). They define the helping task as 'helping clients (their term for the person in need) use their own resources for arriving at their own decisions, to make the best possible choice with respect to whichever personal values and objectives they want to maximize'. They see the helper's task as unmasking the strategy the person uses to avoid making decisions, and suggest that there are four such strategies. These are: (a) unconflicted adherence — the person in need complacently decides to continue whatever they have been doing, ignoring the losses and risks that this involves; (b) unconflicted change to a new course of action — the person in need uncritically adopts a new course of action that seems to them available or is recommended; (c) defensive avoidance — the person in need procrastinates, avoids, blames others and defends and opts for the minimal possible change without reference to the risks or pitfalls of this change; and (d) hyper-vigilance — the person in need searches frantically for a solution to their problem and looks for one which offers immediate relief and then responds to the new situation in just the same way, thereby changing their actions and responses regularly and seemingly randomly. In addition to unmasking these avoidance strategies, the helper has the task of encouraging what Janis and Mann call 'vigilance' — encouraging the person in need to take account of all the relevant information in an unbiased manner and appraising alternative courses of action carefully before deciding on the action to take.

Simply unmasking avoidance and defense strategies does not, however, create goals for the person in need to pursue. To do this, the helper needs to encourage the person in need to define their goal or decision precisely. One way to do this is to ensure that the goal is expressed behaviourally — e.g. 'I will do 4 hours revision each day of the kind we have discussed . . .', or 'I will reduce the number of arguments I have with friends . . .'. Goals, if they are to have an impact on the problem the person in need is experiencing must be realistic — there is no point in developing a goal which cannot be achieved. Helpers have a major task to play in helping the person in need be objective about the goals and decisions they are making whilst at the same time encouraging them to be specific about these goals. One thing that is important in testing the extent to which some goal is realistic is to establish the time frame within which the goal can be acted upon: the longer the time frame the less realistic the goal (Egan 1982).

Some basic educational activities are helpful for educators to engage in during this stage. For example, brainstorming the options open to the person is a useful way of encouraging the person in need to look at options they might not otherwise consider. Checking the information which the person is using as a basis for their decision making and goal setting is also useful — it is sometimes the case that a key piece of information is misunderstood or missing. Finally, the helper should encourage the person in need to evaluate the extent to which the implementation of a decision involves them in risk taking. Whilst risk taking is often necessary if the person is to affect the way they think, feel or relate to others, the risks should be looked at carefully and understood.

The previous sections describing feelings, thoughts and social relationships and the way in which helpers can encourage accurate exploration and understanding by focusing upon them are intended to help the person in need take full account of their situation. In the decision making phase, the helper encourages the person to weigh up in a careful and rational manner the options that are available to them. When helping the person in need to make decisions, the helper needs to encourage them to ask some or all of these questions:

1 Are the risks serious if the person decides not to change in any way and seeks to maintain their present course of action, thinking or feeling?
2 What risks are associated with change (any change)?
3 Is it realistic to hope for a satisfactory alternative to their present state?
4 Is there sufficient time to search for and evaluate the alternatives open to him or her?
5 What gains and losses will accrue to themselves from each of the changes (alternatives) they are considering?
6 How will others be affected by each of the changes (alternatives) that they are considering?
7 In what ways would the choice of a particular course of action (one of the alternatives) lead to self-approval or self-disapproval?
8 In what ways would the choice of a particular course of action (one of the alternatives) lead to increased or decreased social acceptance or approval or disapproval from others who are significant to the person in need?
9 Given responses to questions 1–8, what alternative seems 'best'?
10 Can the best alternative meet all the requirements which the person in need deems to be essential?
11 If the best alternative proves (on the basis of this analysis) to be unsatisfactory, can one of the other options be modified to meet all essential requirements?
12 Once an option is chosen, what are the obstacles to implementing it and letting others know what one is doing?

All of these questions require the helper and the person in need to examine the extent to which a decision or goal is realistic, adequate, clear and likely to affect the situation in which the person finds him or herself. The helper does not work through the list as if it were some kind of checklist — it is more a statement of the kind of issues which need to be explored when the person in need is considering a set of actions.

Presenting these twelve questions in this stark fashion belittles the complexities that the exploration of these questions usually involves. These questions are not easily responded to by many of those in need, and it is this fact that makes this phase of the helper's work most difficult. But it must be undertaken if helping is to be more than developing better understanding (which is sometimes sufficient). The helper encourages adequate appraisal of the challenges faced by the person, assists in the survey of alternatives, helps the person in need weigh up consequences and facilitates the making of a clear decision. They will later have the task of helping the person adhere to that decision, despite negative feedback.

The work in earlier phases of the helping process becomes important at this time. Many of those who seek help continue to 'awfulise' or 'musturbate' when faced with a decision. They also continue to think of consequences in black and white terms, rather than accepting that many of their experiences cannot be characterized in this way. By emphasizing the fact that the person in need can rehearse a decision and its consequences with a helper and develop a more objective view of the alternatives open to them, the helper can fulfil a valuable role at this phase.

ACTION

Once the person in need has come to a decision about what (if anything) they have decided to do, the final task the helper may find themselves pursuing is to support that person in the action they have embarked upon. In a sense, this final phase of helping is concerned with providing continuing objectivity and feedback to the person — helping them accurately to reflect upon and understand what is happening to them and to review events in the light of the preparations the person has made for their actions. Murgatroyd (1985) expressed this role in terms of encouragement, support, nourishment and reflection. The helper should seek to provide a contact point for the person in which they can share what is happening to them in a way that is unique to that helping relationship.

There are a variety of other ways in which the helper can support the person in need when they are trying to change or act in some way. Egan (1982) makes two useful suggestions. One is to point out those features of the situation which are proving supportive and helpful to the person — it should not be assumed that the person in need is always aware of just what is helpful and unhelpful to them. Another is to draw attention to those features of their situation which are detrimental to the achievement of the goals already established.

Indeed, many helpers find that this is the most common task at this stage of the helping process. By looking at the strengths, threats, opportunities and problems inherent in the pursuit of a goal the helper can assist the person in need in the task of monitoring their actions and their consequences.

One other task at this time is to help the person to connect to other supports within their own social group. Friends, relatives, peers and support agencies are all useful sources of support when a person is seeking to implement some sort of decision or initiate some new action. As time passes, the helper should assist the person in need to recognize just who in their social network offers what kind of help and assistance to them and how this help and assistance can best be used without those friends and contacts feeling abused. Pursuing this task is an important way of helping the person in need to go beyond systematic and planned helping (such as that provided by a counsellor) and move to what might be termed 'naturalistic helping' or friendships.

So as to demonstrate the varying tasks of the helper at different stages in the process of helping, sharp distinctions have been drawn in this chapter between the four phases of helping — exploration, understanding, decision making and action. These sharp distinctions are, as was made clear at the beginning of this chapter, artificial. In practice, these phases can take place in sequence, out of sequence, simultaneously or in concatenated form. We draw them out here simply for pedagogic reasons — it helps demonstrate the variety of roles which a helper can play. All require the helper to communicate empathy, warmth and genuineness, and to be as concrete as possible when helping the person in need.

GROUP WORK

Throughout this chapter it has been assumed that the helper is working with an individual on some specific problem or set of problems which that individual feels a need to explore. It is the case, however, that a great deal of helping work with adults takes place in groups. In this short section some points about helping in groups will be examined. The view taken in this chapter is that many of the skills and processes we have described are relevant for group work. Indeed, the phases of helping — exploration, understanding, decision making and action — which we have used to structure the presentation of ideas in this chapter can be seen as a description of the basic stages of group development (Corey 1982).

One thing that is different between working with an individual and working with groups is the level of help available to the individuals within the group. Not only is the helper able to offer support and assistance to group members, so also are others in the group. Indeed, the fact that others in the group are working on their own problems and issues and are critically examining their own understanding of their experiences can mean that the process of helping is made much more poignant and dramatic for the person in need.

In addition to the tasks associated with each of the four phases of helping we have so far described, the helper working in a group has a number of additional tasks. The most critical is to build a sound working relationship both with each member of the group and with the group as a whole. It is vitally important for the well-being of a group which aims to help *all* of its participants that the group leader is seen to be as concerned with each member of the group as he or she is with the group as a whole. One way of doing this is to encourage the group to define its parameters — what it is hoping to achieve, how it will work, the conditions under which individuals can come into and leave the group, etc.. That is, the helper needs to facilitate the negotiation of a contract within the group. Finally, a critical task for the helper is to ensure that members of the group validate and accept each other, even when confronting one another. Members should learn to show and communicate empathy, warmth and genuineness towards their fellow group members.

There are many difficulties associated with running a helping group. One occurs when the group leader has a hidden agenda for the group — one which is not disclosed to the group as a whole. This leads to group members feeling manipulated — the helper is not working with the group but working for the group, seeking to direct its activities. A related concern occurs when the group feels that there is little room for spontaneity — the helper fails to respond creatively and intuitively to the dynamics of the group. A third feature of helping in groups which the helper needs to attend to is the extent to which they are using the group to explore their own needs and problems. Whilst these may be important, group members have come together to look at their needs and difficulties, not those of the helper.

Bearing in mind these points, helping in groups can take a variety of forms. For example, running a study skills workshop or a workshop on coping with examinations or a group on making social relationships can all be regarded as forms of group-based helping. In these groups the various stages of helping we have here outlined will occur, though not necessarily in this order and not at the same pace for each of the persons involved. Indeed, the greater the number involved in a helping activity the more likely it is that the sequencing of the helping process will become confused and that the process will lead into cul-de-sac, hopeless routes and diversions. These all have to be tolerated and learned from. Helping is not a neat and tidy process. This is why it is critical for the helper to develop sound working relationships with each group member.

CASE STUDIES

To put flesh on the bones of the processes we have outlined here, we offer two case studies describing the helping roles played by two different helpers. We present these as illustrations rather than as exemplars or indicative case studies: we make no claim for their typicality either in terms of the specific issue under discussion or in terms of the helping processes used. We present them as cases which illuminate some of the helping practices outlined here.

The first case is that of Miranda, a 28-year-old student of the Open University who is nearing the end of her first year of studying a foundation course in social science. She is extremely worried about her forthcoming examination. She has a series of meetings with her tutor-counsellor, who kept a diary of the work that she did with Miranda. Below we present extracts from that diary.

First contact:
Miranda wanted to talk about exam anxiety. Using three irrational beliefs: (a) I have failed before, therefore I will fail again; (b) I must be competent and achieving at everything in the course otherwise failure is inevitable; and (c) failure will be terrible, awful and impossible to bear. She said that she was so anxious that she couldn't work on her revision and that she didn't really know how to revise. She felt that she was the only one in group with these kinds of problems.

I discussed her irrational beliefs and tried to encourage her to see her beliefs as the source of her anxiety *not* the forthcoming exam. In the tutorial group we discussed the forthcoming exam, and Miranda was helped to realize that all were nervous, some were anxious and that few felt happy about the way their revision was going. I arranged to see Miranda for 15 minutes before the next session.

Second session:
Miranda was waiting for me when I arrived. I helped her unpack her thoughts and feelings more clearly and asked her to decide if she wanted to pass or wanted to continue to expect to fail. She found this a hard question. We looked together at the consequences of her passing and the consequences of her failing and she said that she was definitely going to try to put her past failures behind her and work hard to pass. In the group session that followed we all examined revision techniques and I emphasized the need to select topic areas from within the course (themes) rather than seeking a mastery of all the knowledge presented in the course.

Session three:
Miranda and I met for 15 minutes before the session as planned. She said she was making progress with her studying and revision, but still the thought of the examination made her anxious and she was worried about this. I pointed out that she was now worried about being anxious and that anxiety is the bodily reaction to the repression of some feeling. We did some work on identifying the thoughts and feelings that triggered this anxiety response and she quickly saw how irrational they were — in particular, she recognized that she had begun to awfulize the consequences of failure.

In the group we looked at how we could cope with the day of the examination and stressed the importance of relaxation before the exam, of thoughtful preparation before beginning answering and of checking time and progress.

Last session:
Just one week to go before the examination and Miranda had another 15 minutes before the group session. We quickly went through the revision areas she had covered and I gave re-assurance that she was doing enough work to pass if she decided that she was going to feel in control of herself on the day. I talked her through the way in which she planned to spend the time the day before and on the morning of the examination and she made a list of things to do and thoughts to have.

In the group I went through what happens to the exam paper once the students have completed it and showed a video which describes the lengths the exam boards go to to ensure fairness. All seemed re-assured by this — Miranda, in particular, felt that this had helped her recognize how much passing and failing was in her hands.

Miranda passed her exam, though with only an average grade (which was better than she had originally anticipated). In the space of an hour of private help and about 2 hours of group work, this tutor helped Miranda explore and understand her situation and encouraged her to take responsibility for her thoughts and feelings and their consequences. The tutor used exploration (of thoughts and feelings), understanding (of irrational beliefs and their consequences), decision making (about how to prepare for the last hours before the examination), teaching and information-giving (about the procedures used for marking and about revision), and support as a basis for her helping. Miranda used her time both in private with the tutor-counsellor and in the tutor group to recognize both her own role in creating her distress and the fact that others felt unsure, nervous or anxious too. This was a skilled intervention which lead to Miranda's confidence developing and growing and to her academic success.

Notice that the use of the phases of helping occurred out of sequence in this case — reinforcing the point that helping is a complex and dynamic process that cannot be thought of as a simple series of steps.

The second case study, which again will be presented by means of brief diary entries, concerns John. John is 38 and single. He works as a bank clerk and can readily be described as insular, sensitive and very unsure of himself. At school he obtained eleven 'O' levels and four 'A' levels, three of these latter at grade B. He attended an educational guidance service beause he was thinking of leaving the service of the bank and going to university to read a degree in law. He wanted to see what his options were and how becoming a student would affect him. In the course of talking to the helper at the guidance centre a number of issues were discussed. The extracts are from the helper's case notes.

First session:
John approached the service with a request for information about degrees in law and the financial support for mature students. This we provided quickly, as it is a common request. In talking through the issue with John it soon became clear that he was facing what for him was a difficult decision.
Session two:
John asked for some basic information about becoming a mature student. He was interested in law and the costs of being a student. We examined his motives for wanting to leave work (he worked in a bank) and become a student. He said that he was lonely, frustrated and felt under-used by the bank. He regarded himself as a potential manager, but had not really progressed very far since he started work.
We explored what leaving work and becoming a student of law would mean. Each time we looked at a difficulty (e.g. paying the rent, study skills, support for his work) he suggested that it would all be worth it in the end. He wanted to specialize in corporate law and would soon be earning big money after he had graduated. I explained that a first degree in law did not entitle him to practise at the bar (this is what

he wanted) — he would have to sit bar exams, eat dinners in one of the law temples in London and undertake a period as an apprentice. This came as a surprise to John who did not fully realize what was involved. He also had unreal expectations about how much money he would get as a student — it made him think about this course of action carefully.

Session three:

John had thought about doing law as a part-time student with the Open University, but had found out that this is one of the subjects not offered by them. He also had decided against doing a law degree as an external student at the University of London — everyone had told him how hard it was. He now felt he didn't really know what he wanted to do, only that he had to do something.

We made a list of the reasons why he felt that he needed to do something. It became clear that he had no hobbies and hardly any social life. His life revolved around his work. I said I found this surprising and felt that he would, given his age, have developed a range of hobbies and interests. He said, interestingly, that he 'had never needed to'. When asked what this meant, he said that there was no point in having a hobby unless it led to something.

We spent some time looking at the difference between extrinsic and intrinsic motivation. It was clear that John had not thought of himself as only interested in rewards offered by others and had never really looked carefully at the internal satisfactions that can come from doing a job well, trying out a new activity, meeting new people and so on. I asked him to draw up a list of things he would be willing to try in an attempt to obtain some internal satisfactions.

Session four:

John's list was interesting. For a start, there was no mention of law or legal studies. Indeed, of the list of six things only one could be regarded as academic — developing language skills in French. Top of the list was learning more about wine and food.

I drew John's attention to the existence of several wine/food courses and clubs in the area. He expressed some slight interest — if anything he seemed unsure just why he was coming to the guidance service. I wrote out a list of food/wine courses for him.

Session five (one month after Session four):

John came in to thank me. He had decided, much to his own surprise he said, to go to a wine appreciation course at a local adult education centre. He was welcomed on the course and was surprised to see 18 other people there. Everyone seemed friendly and he had met a very nice couple and a lady and had been out for a meal with the three of them. The class was planning a trip to the Rhone valley for a wine-tasting holiday. He was sure he was going to go on it.

What's more, he had also enrolled for a class about Italian art. He found this very stimulating and again the people were friendly, though not as friendly as those in the wine class. I asked him about work and he said that now he had other interests things felt better at work. He also

said that he had decided that, at his age, he was no longer ambitious —
just restless, and that these were not the same thing. We explored this
idea for some time (about 20 minutes). What became clear was that
John's initial request was not actually as specific as it sounded: he
wanted to feel good about something and when he first came in he was
feeling good about the fantasy of being a successful corporate lawyer.
In the light of day and being helped to think it through, he now felt good
about knowing a little more about wine, having some new friends and
going to a class. He said that though these things sounded small in
comparison with the idea of reading for a law degree, they were in fact
having a significant effect on him.

Last session:

It is 5 months since John last came in to see us. He says that he wants to
do a course on management — the bank are taking more interest in him
now — and that he really wants to show them that he's interested in
them but does not want to do anything too demanding. I told him about
the distance-based teaching programmes offered by Strathclyde and
the Open University and he was interested in these and might pursue
them. I also told him about some shorter management events — 1-day,
2-day and 5-day events — in which he expressed most interest, especially those offered by the Manchester Business School. I asked him if
this was another enquiry like the one about law. He smiled, and said
'No, things have changed a lot since then'. He was now dating the girl
from the wine class and together they were going to Italy this summer
for a holiday so that they could look at some of the paintings that he had
been learning about. Because he felt he had her companionship, he felt
more comfortable about his job and had started to apply for promotion.
Things looked to be going well. He had enrolled for a cookery course
with his lady friend and they were thinking of doing some management
education together.

John's presenting issue — feeling restless about his situation and
wanting to do something — is a common presenting issue in educational guidance services (see Chapter 6). What is interesting about
this case is that it involved the helper in working with John to explore
the real needs he was expressing and in encouraging an understanding of these needs. The helper did little more. There was also a
false start — the question of the law degree — and some need for
reality testing about being a full-time mature student and becoming a
corporate lawyer. The helper's major skills were listening and
enabling John to better understand his own needs. John made his
own decisions and took his own actions — he used the helper for
exploration and understanding.

We do not suggest that helpers reading these cases should feel that
they are cases that they should, as a result of reading this book, be

able to handle. The point of presenting them is to give a clear idea of how helping occurs in practice. We also want to encourage the idea that helping takes place in a variety of ways — not always as systematic as the schema we have used in this chapter would suggest. It is often a messy process with false starts (as in the case of John) and with the phases of helping out of sequence (as with Miranda). In both cases, the helper developed a working relationship with the person in need so as to facilitate some action that helped them with a specific problem that concerned them.

SOME POINTS FOR THE HELPER

Not all helpers have the time, organizational support or skills to undertake helping that involves the kind of time and energy which the cases of Miranda and John involved. Yet, Miranda and John could each be helped by a number of people in a variety of different ways. Helpers need to recognize their own skills and limitations and work within them (Corey 1982; Murgatroyd 1985). The following five points are useful reminders that helpers need to learn about themselves through their work as helpers:

1 I can do no more than my best — you can always imagine others doing different and perhaps better things when helping the person in need. But if you are doing your best and are seeking to learn from the experience in as many ways as possible, then you can do no more.

2 Being anxious about helping is normal: being concerned about the quality of the helping one is offering or about its consequences is normal for a helper (irrespective of the training they have received). Use this anxiety or concern as a spur to your learning about the process of helping.

3 The helper cannot be perfect: you can expect to make mistakes; you should want to learn from them in a way that ensures that you continue to develop your skills and abilities as a helper. You cannot be thoroughly competent and achieving at everything all the time.

4 Instant results are impossible: there are no instant cures or potions, magic formulae or spells that a helper can cast. Significant changes take time. Rather than looking for cures and outcomes, attend to the process of helping.

5 You will not succeed with everyone who seeks your help: no

matter how good you are and how many courses you have attended, you will not be able to help all those who seek your help. Recognize your limitations and work to move your own skills forward. If in doubt, find others who can help.

These five points are reiterated here because all helpers need to recognize the importance of their own learning during helping. These points can act as powerful reminders of the frailty of one person seeking to help another; they also remind us of the importance of trying.

Helping is a function of the skills and experience of the helper. But it is also constrained by other factors, most particularly the nature of the organization in which the helper's work is taking place. For example, many of those who work in education as helpers complain that they lack the proper facilities — a quiet room, time and secretarial support — to help those in need in the way that they would like. Others suggest that the particular organization in which they work imposes constraints — e.g. about the kinds of problems that they are allowed to offer help with. For example, the MSC Youth Training Scheme has a specific time within its programme for counselling young people in terms of job-related and life-skills needs — such time is not always allocated within an FE college offering apprenticeship programmes in association with a local company. In some organizations, individuals are sent to a helper involuntarily whilst in others help seeking is always a voluntary act. These institutional differences can affect the ability of the helper to be effective in their own terms. The fact that these institutional constraints exist makes the list of five points above more relevant. For they remind the helper of their own limitations and constraints.

CONCLUSION

This chapter has indicated the areas of skill which a helper needs to develop if they are to provide systematic helping services to those in need. Using the ideas and frameworks of the previous chapter, we have suggested that helping can be conceived of as a process in which the helper seeks to help the person in need explore, understand, and come to terms with their situation. We have also suggested that the helper should seek to encourage the person to think through and act upon a decision about their situation and support them in living through the consequences of their actions. Two case studies of helping — one involving an adult educator and the other a volunteer helper — have been used to illustrate just how these objectives can be achieved. Throughout we have stressed the importance of empathy, warmth, genuineness and concreteness as the basis on which the particular phases and skills of helping are achieved.

Later chapters of this book develop these ideas further in a variety of contexts.

Continuing Education: Learning and Teaching in Groups

INTRODUCTION

This chapter looks at the process of helping in the context of education for adults. In the United Kingdom there is a wide variety of educational provision which embraces a broad spectrum of topics at different levels from basic to intermediate to post-graduate, and it is provided by different organizations in a variety of settings, such as schools, colleges, community centres, and places of employment. It is possible to join vocational courses, professional updating courses, courses orientated towards citizenship and community welfare, courses associated with leisure, cultural and recreational activities, and so on. Providers include universities, colleges of further and higher education, local education authorities, professional associations, vocational training agencies such as the Manpower Services Commission, voluntary associations, community associations, employers, etc.. This variety is illustrated by, for example, Percy *et al*. (1983) in their study of Post-initial Education in the North-West of England.

Adult education is not, like education for children, an integral part of state provision. Piecemeal development has taken place over the years as different groups and organizations have become interested in educating adults, and adults have demanded opportunities to continue their education. The distribution of provision as a result is not uniform and duplications and gaps in provision exist. Nevertheless, there are now over the country a variety of opportunities for adults to continue their education, and many do so at one time, or frequently, during their lives.

It was suggested in Chapter 2 that basic principles of helping which apply to counselling apply also to other forms of helping, and this chapter seeks to show how they are relevant to the process of teaching adults. The process of teaching/learning is often regarded only in terms of giving/receiving information, but as more knowledge is gained about it it becomes evident that it is far more complex than this. There follows a consideration of the process of learning in adults, which takes up and develops in terms of educational settings some of the points made about learning in the first three chapters. This leads into a discussion of implications for the process of teaching adults. The discussion is in general terms and is of relevance to many different types of education for adults. The variety of courses available is so wide, however, that it cannot be claimed to be equally applicable to all of them. The emphasis in this chapter lies towards those with a relatively high academic content. The discussion as a whole is perhaps best looked on as an exploration into some aspects of a complex topic, and as suggesting broad guidelines. There is still a great deal to be learnt about the needs and characteristics of adult learners and about ways in which to facilitate their learning (Millard 1981; Hounsell 1984).

LEARNING IN ADULT LIFE

Throughout their lives adults experience changes with which they have to find ways of coping. They are capable during most, if not all, their lifespan of altering perspectives from which they view themselves and their environments, and of thinking, feeling and acting in new ways. It was pointed out in Chapter 2 that thinking, feeling and acting are closely interlinked in all of us, and that if we concentrate on learning how to change along one of these dimensions then the other two are likely to be affected as well. In adult education the emphasis is often on the cognitive dimension, that is acquiring more information about a particular topic or a particular activity or skill, and this may alter how we feel and act. For example, we may feel differently about the respective roles of men and women in society if we make a study of this topic, and this may lead us to alter ways in which we interact with the opposite sex.

There is some debate about how intellectual functioning changes over a lifespan, as was pointed out in Chapter 1. However, some adults well into old age want to and are able to succeed in sophisticated learning projects. The Open University, for example, has had some students in their eighties who have successfully completed a degree course. It is rather unfortunate that there is a conventional wisdom which is still widespread that the ageing process must inevitably be accompanied by intellectual decline. It is not unusual to hear adults from their forties upwards expressing doubts about undertaking courses in continuing education because they fear that they may be 'past it'!

It is of importance to note that adults are not necessarily dependent on 'experts' in formal organizations for help in continuing their education any more than they are when seeking ways to cope with personal problems. During the course of their lives, without any contact with educational institutions, they may take up many personal learning projects with the deliberate intention of bringing about change in knowledge, attitudes or skills. Finding out about these projects is not very easy because of their individual and private nature. Some research has been done — by, for example, Tough (1971). It would appear from Tough's study, and subsequent ones, that almost every adult undertakes one or two learning projects every year, with eight not being uncommon. The learner plans the programme of learning and may seek help from friends, acquaintances, written sources, audio-visual sources, and so on. It is possible to learn about, say, how to create a rock garden, how to make homemade wine, how to paper a room, how to service a car, or perhaps find out more about astronomy, or local history, or some aspect of child development. The possibilities are very wide indeed. Many people undertake such activities without describing them as learning projects, or even thinking of them in terms of 'continuing education'.

Adults are unlikely to carry on learning at the same rate throughout their lives, whether on an informal or formal basis. Informal individual projects are taken up and put down, and adults may move in and out of the continuing education sector one or many times during the course of their lives. Whether learning takes place in formal or informal settings, it has been suggested, it can be described as 'an ebb and flow of repeated progression and regression, according to a complex interplay between the individual and his environment, until (and if) critical biological decay intrudes towards the end of the lifespan' (Giles and Woolfe 1981, p. 36). Individuals are likely to give particular attention to the nature of this interplay between the self and the environment when they experience changes in their lives. These might be major changes, such as getting married and setting up home, which could provide an incentive for learning something about DIY, or changing jobs, which might involve learning new information and different skills. Or changes might be on a more minor scale, such as purchasing a word processor and then learning how to use it, or deciding to go for a holiday in a foreign country and taking steps to learn something of the language before setting out. In order to cope with the variety in life it would appear that many people from time to time experience a need to continue their education, and they take steps to satisfy that need.

Amongst adults motivations for learning and expectations about outcomes are very varied, as was suggested in Chapter 1 and they may often have more than one reason for entering formal education. A useful concept which embraces the collection of purposes which any one person may bring is that of 'educational orientation' (Gibbs *et al.*, 1984). Orientation is described as the quality of the relationship between the learner and a course. It is a way of describing an adult's context for studying and the personal framework to which learning is related and through which it acquires meaning. It might be predominantly vocational, to gain an appropriate qualification or training; it might be primarily academic, that is, an interest in the subject matter for its own sake or in the process of studying for its own sake; possibly it is the personal aspect which is most important, and the individual concerned wants to prove that he or she is really capable of studying, or wishes to widen his or her horizons on life; or perhaps the emphasis is on the social side, that is, study as a recreation and in the company of other people. The vocational element is likely to be most important more often amongst lower age groups, and the social element may well be more noticeable on certain courses, such as leisure activities. In any one group of learners, however, there will probably be considerable variety in the nature of their educational orientations.

Sometimes adults want to concentrate on learning in the very short term, that is, on remembering some facts or acquiring new skills in a mechanical fashion, as in learning to play a TV quiz game. Such learning may serve a particular purpose, for instance, relaxation from more pressing matters in life. The term 'learning' in this chapter, however, and indeed in the book as a whole, concentrates on a wider and deeper process of understanding for the long term. People can use this type of learning to build on their existing understanding and experiences, and to interpret and re-interpret life. They are thereby able, in the words of Chapter 2, to place themselves in a new relationship to themselves and/or to the world in which they live.

APPROACHES TO THE LEARNING PROCESS

Adults develop a range of attitudes towards and skills in learning, and these are likely to differ from one person to another along a number of dimensions. Marton and Saljo (1984, p. 37) have pointed out that if the outcome of learning in terms of understanding differs between individuals, then the very process of learning which leads to different outcomes must also have differed. It is inaccurate to try to explain differences in outcome simply in terms of the people concerned being 'lazy' or 'not very bright'. The following discussion draws on the findings of a few investigations in order to direct attention to several interconnected aspects of the learning process.

Conceptions of the learning process

One aspect is that of the degree of sophistication which an individual has attained with regard to conceptions of the learning process itself. Saljo (1979), for example, carried out an interview study in which he asked a group of adults what learning meant to them, and analysis of the transcripts produced five qualitatively different conceptions: a quantitative increase in knowledge; memorizing; the acquisition of facts, methods etc. which can be retained and used when necessary; the abstraction of meaning; and an interpretative process aimed at understanding reality. The way in which the adults went about reading an article seemed to mirror these conceptions. Some of the adults, it would appear, regarded learning in more complex terms than did others.

An alternative approach to this aspect of the learning process is that of Bloom (1956) (as interpreted by Fontana 1982, p. 291), who suggests it is possible to conceive of a hierarchy of thinking skills. From the simplest to the most complex, these are as follows: knowledge (of facts, terms etc.); comprehension (an understanding of the meaning of the knowledge); application (ability to apply knowledge and comprehension in new and concrete situations); analysis (ability to break down knowledge into constituent parts and to see the relationships between them); synthesis (ability to judge the value of material using explicit and coherent criteria, either of one's own devising or derived from the work of others). Each of the higher levels subsumes those inferior to it.

Perry (1970) has produced a nine-stage model of intellectual and ethical development through which, he suggests, adults move as they develop their conception of learning. The adult at stage one adopts a passive accepting role to learning, believing all questions have simple answers which are right or wrong. As the adult moves along the road to intellectual maturity he or she comes to accept diversity and uncertainty as legitimate, and by stage 5 recognizes that knowledge and values are relative, contingent and contextual. An adult who reaches stage 9 is ready to commit the self to a personal inter-pretation of knowledge, and to integrate his or her learning in the responsible interpretation of personal life. The way in which adults perceive learning tasks, Perry suggests, is limited by the stage of development which they have reached. For example, if a lecturer announces he or she will consider three theories, learner A, who assumes knowledge consists of correct answers, waits for the lecturer to state which theory should be learnt. Learner B, who believes the same but knows that tutors sometimes present problems so that the audience can find the right answers, sees the lecture as a kind of guessing game. Learner C assumes an answer can be called 'right' only in the light of its context, and that several interpretations may be legitimate, depending on the angle of approach. That learner there-fore expects three legitimate theories to be examined for their strong and weak points.

It may be that this particular scheme of Perry's is more relevant to learners in the arts and humanities than to those in mathematical, scientific and technological fields, as Entwistle (1981) suggests, and perhaps the latter group require a modified scheme. Nevertheless, this does not negate the notion of the concept of learning becoming more sophisticated as an adult moves towards intellectual maturity.

Learning strategies

When faced with a learning task, it is necessary for an adult to find a strategy to cope with it. Different researchers have put forward different ways of conceptualizing such strategies. For example, Pask and Scott (1972) have distinguished between 'serialists' and 'holists'. Serialists are step by step learners who build understanding out of component details, connecting them together one after another in order to reach more general principles. Holists are global learners who seek to build up from the start a broad view of a learning task and look for relationships between ideas and seek interconnections with other topics, filling in details bit by bit.

Marton (1975) also has a bi-polar concept relating to the processing of information. He has distinguished between surface level and deep level processing. Surface learners assimilate knowledge in the form in which it is presented to them, and focus their attention on learning specific pieces of information. Those who adopt deep level processing are concerned about the logic of arguments, the assumptions and values on which arguments rest, and are prepared to question conclusions and to relate the information to previous knowledge. How this processing reveals itself in practice may vary according to the nature of the subject matter. For example, a deep approach to the humanities is typified by an intention from the outset to reinterpret the material in a personal way, while in the sciences an initial concentration on details is often indispensable to a deep approach (Hounsell 1984).

Other researchers have investigated how students cope with a course as a whole. For example, Parlett (1970) has described some learners as syllabus bound; they prefer to work within the confines of a syllabus, with clear instructions and deadlines. There are other learners who are 'syllabus free' who seek much more autonomy in learning and have intellectual interests which may run far beyond the syllabus. Miller and Parlett (1974) have distinguished three groups: these are cue-seekers i.e. those who actively seek to elicit from their tutors an understanding of the structure of the course; cue-conscious learners who are able to pick up hints about the structure which are passed on by tutors; and cue-deaf learners who do not respond to information about structure.

Study skills

The way in which adults practise study skills is likely to be influenced by stages reached in intellectual maturity and by strategies adopted. For instance, the notes taken by the three learners in the Perry example would probably show considerable differences. It is not only the possession of a range of tactics which is important in order to practise study skills satisfactorily, which is why although study skills booklets may offer useful suggestions and ideas they cannot provide easy solutions to how to learn more effectively. If learners concentrate on improving their skills, however, in relation to the course which they are studying this may in turn lead them to think further about strategies and attitudes towards the whole process of learning.

Adults who come to continuing education may need to learn some new skills, and they may be glad of help in applying their existing skills, for example, in reading, writing, and note taking, in a way appropriate to the educational setting. For instance, they may seek to learn a variety of ways in which to present coherent arguments, to read at different speeds, to improve powers of concentration, to improve the ability to organize and use time effectively, to make better use of group discussions, to improve the skill of listening, and so on.

There is no one right or best way at a tactical level of practising most study skills. In a group of learners listening to the same lecture, for example, there are likely to be as many different forms of notes produced as there are people taking them. Perhaps some learners write down only a few key words or phrases, some may have a neat arrangement of major headings and subheadings, some may have a collection of words and phrases with a system of arrows indicating interconnections between points, and others may write notes in the form of a diagram. Similarly, given the same article, some learners may scan it, others skim it, and others read it much more slowly word for word.

The path of learning

It is not difficult to see that the particular combination of degree of intellectual maturity, types of strategies and range of study skills and tactics brought by each adult to the task of study is likely to be unique to that person. It has been suggested that the more sophisticated learners are those who are moving along the path to increased intellectual maturity, are increasing the range of strategies, skills and tactics at their disposal, and are becoming more expert in using them flexibly in order to obtain maximum advantage for them personally out of any learning opportunity they may have. For example, when approaching a topic for the first time some versatile learners may consciously choose to adopt a surface approach, at least until some understanding of essential concepts and terminology has been gained, and do not become over-anxious about not being able to grasp all arguments immediately. Howe (1976) puts it in terms of the so-called 'good learner' having a set of intellectual skills that vary in function and complexity, so that when faced with a new task he or she is likely to have available a greater or more effective repertoire of procedures and strategies than the so-called 'poor learner'. Beard (1976) likens the good learner to an explorer who uses his or her ingenuity to deal with the unexpected, who is flexible when facing new circumstances, and is able to obtain relevant information.

Adults have personal resources which they can use on their path of learning. They also have internal resistances with which they have to cope. In addition they may experience environmental influences as supportive, or as constraints which may be modified or to which it is necessary to adapt. These internal and external influences also affect the approaches of adults to learning, and will be looked at briefly in the next two sections.

MOVING TOWARDS A NEW RELATIONSHIP WITH THE SELF

There are in our inner worlds not only resources but also constraints, intellectual and emotional, which influence the learning process. There is much to be learnt yet about just how this internal learning process takes place. In general terms, however, it seems true to say that incoming information in the present is interpreted in terms of previous knowledge and experience. Most individuals desire constancy, and tend to resist interference from competing information which disturbs their 'set' or filing system or chains of associations which they have built up inside themselves, and which help to give order and stability to their lives. Beard (1976) suggests in the light of available evidence that people differ in their capacity to relinquish 'sets', some doing so fairly readily, whereas others distort information which they receive, forcing it to fit familiar interpretations until the weight of contradictions may oblige them to change.

Often new learning, whether about a particular topic or about how to perform a skill, is relatively easily assimilated and reinforces, or requires only a slight modification to, the internal filing system. When there is resistance, More (1974) has put forward a suggestion about the nature of the process which takes place. There is first of all a stage of intellectual awareness of new knowledge. This is followed by emotional responses, and then ever increasing awareness of these responses as they are brought to the level of the intellect. The intellectual and emotional interplay which follows may last minutes, days, weeks, months or even years, and operates against the background of the learner's life situation. Sometimes the conflict remains unresolved and ways have to be found of tolerating it. Most students, however, according to More, bring themselves through to the final stage, the resolution of learning conflict. The learning has then truly become part of themselves, and they are ready for more learning.

This learning process may be accompanied by a whole range of emotions, such as anxiety, anger, and depression before the new knowledge is finally assimilated. It is sometimes analagous to the process of grieving referred to in Chapter 1. It is possible to experience acutely the loss of a long-held cherished belief or customary way of thinking, acting or feeling, as it is possible to experience acutely the death of a close relative, or end of a marriage, and so on, although the scale might be different. And this transition phase may be difficult even when the new information or skills are very much desired.

An example of initial resistance to change comes from a workshop which was run on helping skills for student health visitors. All of them were trained nurses, and such training is conducive to the development of an approach to patients which emphasizes the need to soothe and comfort. In the course of role play, the possibility of a health visitor helping her clients by using confrontation was raised. This tactic might be useful, or even necessary, it was suggested, if there were, say, discrepancies in what clients said at different times, or if they constantly avoided discussing topics painful to them. The notion of confrontation was greeted with incredulity and even anger by a few of the students, for it challenged values and assumptions very important to them about how they believed they should tackle their work (Rhys 1986).

Some people may perhaps go part-way through the process of absorbing new information and then decide not to go any further, and reject or only partly assimilate it (Perry 1970; More 1974). It may seem too dangerous or perhaps too much of an effort to give up the familiar and accept the unfamiliar.

It is possible that earlier learning experiences have not prepared adults for handling independently experiences in learning. Anxiety about many aspects of learning is not uncommon. There may be general lack of confidence in the self and an unrealistic appraisal of personal abilities and intellectual products (Stanton 1981; Powell 1981). Nelson-Jones (1982) considers what he terms a 'sense of learning competence' an important factor in the learning process. This is a comprehensive term which recognizes that there are emotional, motivational and interest variables in learning. He suggests that a lack of sense of learning competence may inhibit learners from realizing *actual* competence, whether in examinations, reading, note taking, use of study time, creativity, critical thinking, etc.. It is a subjective feeling. The same grade for an essay, for example, might be regarded with pleasure as an achievement by one learner, and with a sense of despair by another. If they are to move forward learners need to gain increasing trust in their own judgements and abilities and become more able to weigh up their strengths and weaknesses as dispassionately as possible.

One message which can be drawn from the available evidence on how people cope intellectually and emotionally with their learning is that for an adult one important facet of the overall process may well be coming to understand how to mobilize more effectively inner resources to cope with inner constraints.

COPING WITH THE ENVIRONMENT

It is possible to mention here only a few features of the social and physical environment which may influence the approach of adults to the process of learning. It has been suggested that there are different systems in our environments which are needed for support, challenge, and so on, at different stages in our life development, ranging from the close immediate personal setting to the wider cultural milieu (Egan and Cowan 1979). The relative importance of constraints in these different systems is similarly likely to vary over time.

The nature of the course a learner is studying may sometimes be to some extent an immediate source of constraint. Many courses are, as far as the learner is concerned, tutor prescribed, tutor presented, tutor paced and tutor assessed. Tutors may be acting independently, or, more often, in response to criteria laid down about the course by the institutions which employ them. It may be necessary, for instance, to cover a certain syllabus within a specified time, and prepare learners for examinations and/or methods of continuous assessment. How a learner approaches the task of learning is influenced, perhaps strongly, by how he or she interprets such rules and regulations. Gibbs *et al.* (1982, p. 25) suggest 'the most powerful and pervasive influence on student learning is the curriculum and its assessment'. If the curriculum is heavy, time short, assessment rigorous, and succeeding in the course very important to a learner, then it is very likely he or she will concentrate on surface learning and direct all efforts towards passing the assessment, not towards learning for the long term.

Not all courses in continuing education are surrounded by so many strictures. There are courses, for instance, at the Schools of Independent Studies at Lancaster University and the North East London Polytechnic, in which learners are given only a general indication of what to do within a certain time limit, and, in conjunction with one or more members of staff, they work out for themselves a syllabus, mode of study, and so on. Some Open University courses take the form of 'guided learning', and a considerable number include projects which the learners themselves choose. This notion of project is used in many other types of settings, for example, courses in photography and art.

Even if regulations are strict, there is usually some room for tutors to choose how to teach. Some researchers, such as Ramsden (1979), Laurillard (1984), have pointed out the influence that the attitude a tutor has towards subject matter and the teaching strategies and tactics employed can have on learners. More will be said about this in the discussion on teaching later in the chapter.

The social context in which the learning takes place may also be important. The climate prevailing in a group can help or hinder learning and can influence the nature of interrelationships which develop between group members and how they use opportunities which they may have for giving help to and receiving help from one another. In addition, physical conditions for a group may be very pleasant, but sometimes learners have to cope with uncomfortable seating, or draughty or stuffy rooms, which are not conducive to study.

Constraints in the wider environment may also influence the learning process. Some adults may be restricted in when they study and how much time they can devote to it by work and/or family commitments, or perhaps there are financial or transport difficulties, and so on. The cultural milieu in which they move may or may not encourage learning by adults. For example, there may be political pressures on 16-year-old school leavers to continue with their education, whereas women with families who return to study may sometimes be accused of neglecting their home commitments; widespread unemployment and the uncertainty of being able to obtain a job even with additional qualifications can affect the motivations of some learners.

THE LEARNER AS AN INDIVIDUAL

The evidence suggests that educational orientation, approach to learning, and the experience of constraints, both internal and external, in combination inform the way in which an adult copes with continuing education. Perhaps there are many forces pushing a person in one direction. For example, someone with a vocational extrinsic orientation whose primary objective is to pass a course may be content to regard learning primarily as the acquisition of facts, stick to surface-level processing, and the minimum of study skills and tactics necessary to get by, while keeping an ear open for useful hints a tutor might offer; he or she would probably not be too bothered by internal resistances because the new knowledge is regarded primarily as a means to an end, and would be willing to accept departmental rules and regulations about the syllabus, and so on. But the complexities of the learning process are such that there is considerable potential for learners to find themselves subject to conflicting pressures. For instance, the person who prefers to be syllabus-free is likely to find authoritarian regulations irksome; someone experiencing an emotional blockage may become increasingly anxious if work and domestic pressures make finding time for quiet reflection difficult; a learner who has long accepted the relative and contextual nature of knowledge may experience boredom and isolation in a group in which other members are moving only slowly away from more simplistic approaches.

Each learner has to sort out his or her own personal path of learning; no one else can do it on behalf of that person, although other people can offer help on the way. Decisions have to be constantly made about how to interpret a learning situation and its requirements, about which strategies to use, which tactics to employ, and so on. The process any person goes through in coming to those decisions most appropriate for him or her can be conceived of as having four stages. First there is the stage of awareness, awareness of resources and opportunities and constraints which emanate from within the self and from the environment. Entwistle (1981, p. 269) suggests that for tutors 'the effort to raise student "awareness" of their own approaches and strategies may be the single most effective way of raising general levels of understanding'. The second stage is that of evaluating those factors. The third is looking at options which are open for action and choosing amongst them, and the fourth is to translate that option into action, and have the courage and determination to do so. These stages are very similar to those outlined in connection with counselling in Chapters 2 and 3. It is suggested that they are as valid a way of analyzing the process of learning in educational settings as in settings in which the focus of attention is on personal problems.

This discussion on learning has necessarily been brief, but perhaps enough has been said to indicate that the approach of any one person is likely to be a composite which consists of a wide range of variables, some of which have been touched on in this discussion. Because the learning process is so complex, then it follows that the process of teaching must also be complex. Attention is now turned to some implications complexities of the process of learning have for the process of teaching and how basic principles of helping which apply to counselling are relevant to teaching.

THE PERSONAL CONTEXT OF TEACHING

One of the ingredients of the process of teaching is the meaning the occupation of teaching holds for the tutor. The concept of educational orientation was used when discussing the learning process in adults to describe the nature of the relationship between the learner and a course. It is possible to use a similar sort of concept, which may be called occupational orientation, to describe the personal context of a tutor with regard to teaching. Like educational orientation it may vary in content at different times during a tutor's career, the variations being associated with changes in the tutor and in the environment, and like educational orientation it can be subdivided into four different elements: vocational, academic, personal and social. There are possibilities of wide variation in the relative importance and nature of each element from one tutor to another, as the following paragraphs indicate.

It was explained in the introduction that the nature of the education available for adults is very varied, and it is taught by many different types of tutors. Some are employed full time, and it is their means of livelihood. Some are employed part time from one or two hours a week, to perhaps two or three days a week, and they may or may not have another occupation. Some tutors work on a casual basis, and yet others on a voluntary basis and are not paid for their services. It is not possible to make any generalizations about how important as a vocation teaching adults is likely to be. Some who work full time, for instance, may not feel very committed to it as an occupation in itself, while to some part-time and voluntary tutors it may be a very important aspect of their lives.

The academic element also varies from one person to another. Some tutors are deeply involved in their subject areas, taking every opportunity to increase their knowledge and skills, perhaps also undertaking research and contributing to the literature through books and articles. Similarly, some are very interested in the teaching process for its own sake. For others it may be a case of concentrating only on the subject matter relevant for their courses, keeping up to date as necessary, and taking the process of teaching more or less for granted.

It is a theme of this chapter, and of the book, that becoming more skilful in the process of helping others requires the helper to be willing and able to develop as a thinking, feeling and doing being. How, and the extent to which, a tutor develops this personal element through the teaching process is open to wide differences between tutors. This applies also to the social element. For some tutors, teaching is work and is set apart from social life with family and friends. For others, social contact with colleagues may be important. For yet others, the process of interacting with both learners and fellow tutors may be a very significant element in their lives, and perhaps a way of building up a friendship network.

APPROACHES TO TEACHING

At the end of Chapter 2, following the discussion on counselling, it was suggested that there are three groups of questions which helpers might ask themselves about three different dimensions of the helping process. These can usefully be adapted to the process of teaching. They focus respectively on (a) the individual characteristics of learners and the relationship of the tutor to them as individuals;

(b) the development of a learning group as a unit, and relationships within it; and (c) the qualities and skills of the tutor as a person. It is suggested, however, that a fourth dimension which is implicit in the discussion on counselling should be separated out in the case of teaching, that is, (d) the handling of information, not least because the raison d'être of adult education at a societal level is the provision of opportunities for adults to improve knowledge about particular topics and skills. It is not being suggested that these are the only possible dimensions; they are, however, important considerations and central to this discussion of the teaching process as a form of helping, and they will now be considered in turn (with (c) and (d) in reverse order).

Individual learners

It has been suggested in this chapter that each adult follows his or her own unique path of learning, and that there are many differences possible in motivations, aspirations, attitudes, intellectual maturity, study strategies, and so on, which individuals bring to their learning, and also in the inner and external resources and constraints with which they are living. If this is accepted, it follows that any group of learners is characterized by heterogeneity, not homogeneity. A tutor has to take initiatives to get to know learners as individuals and how they approach their learning, as far as is practicable in the prevailing circumstances, if the process of facilitating their learning is to be as helpful to them as possible. For example, the learner who regards studying a course as an important contribution to his or her career may well have a different approach to course content and study method from someone whose interest is in the subject matter and in studying for their own sake.

It would seem important, however, for tutors to try to find a balance between trying to do too much to help learners, 'spoon feeding' as it is sometimes called, which inhibits the development of autonomy, and turning a blind eye to learners' difficulties, which leaves them floundering with cognitive and/or emotional blockages and/or practical difficulties in relation to the course itself or to external constraints. Part of the process of teaching is, in Bramley's words (1979, p. 48) 'sensitizing individual participants to recognize and own their autonomy', and then helping them to develop and extend their personal resources for learning.

Not all adults, of course, require the same amount of help. For example, some may enter courses already possessing a wide range of relevant learning skills and knowledge; and others may decide that their ways of learning are sufficiently satisfactory to get by and they do not wish to accept opportunities to extend them. The process of helping involves negotiation between tutor and learner.

Group development

Learners are important as individuals, and they are also important as a collective. The tutor is not their only helper. Learners can help one another, provided they are given opportunities and encouragement to do so. It is possible as the group develops as a unit to conceive of the teaching/learning process taking on the character of a kind of conversation in which students' thinking and ideas are continuously utilized as a means of moving forward (Holmberg 1984). If learners are taking an active part in the learning experience of a group, and sharing responsibility for it, this may well help to increase their feeling of commitment. One of the skills in teaching is to make the most of group potential.

It is as important in teaching as in counselling to pay attention to the group climate. In traditional authoritarian classroom settings permitted types of self-expression are normally very restricted. If adults are going to develop competence intellectually and emotionally, however, they need to feel safe enough to express a wide range of ideas, thoughts and feelings without fear of shame or of being made to look ridiculous. Some adults hesitate about voicing disagreements with other people's opinions and ideas, or expressing negative feelings about any type of information with which they may be presented, and it may take some time to overcome such barriers. Perry (1970) in the course of his research was interested in how much the learners he studied valued support and community, and they came to realize that the risks and individuality of learning were the same not only for themselves but also for their tutors.

Handling information

It is normally assumed that a tutor should be well acquainted with and up to date in his or her topic. Perhaps not quite so much importance is always attached to the ability to put it across in different ways to meet the varying needs of learners. For example, a teaching method which holists or global learners find useful may leave serialists or step by step learners somewhat bemused. There may be blockages in understanding, both cognitive and emotional, which may have a variety of causes. For example, an explanation of a particular theory which some learners find helpful may leave others puzzled, perhaps because they do not have an essential piece of prior knowledge on which to hook this new information, or perhaps they have misunderstood the definitions of some essential concept, or perhaps they feel reluctant to accept the theory because it appears to contradict some preconceived notions. Part of the process of teaching is to keep checking on learners' understanding and to do it in such a way that it does not cause shame or embarrassment, and then to respond to any difficulties there may be. Tutors need a range of strategies and tactics on which to draw to be able to do this.

Blockages may also be related to uncertainties on the part of learners about how to handle information. It has been suggested that stages of intellectual maturity, strategies for studying and the ways in which study skills are practised are intimately related one with another. Difficulties may have their source in any of these areas. It may sometimes be that the most effective form of help that tutors can give is to explore one or more aspects of the learning process with individuals or a group as a whole, using the subject matter as a means of carrying this out. Indeed, the ability and willingness to do this would seem to be essential if tutors are to help people develop as learners in the long term.

The tutor as a person

If tutors are to relate to learners as individuals and to the group as a unit, and are to encourage the development of a climate of safety, and handle information sensitively with regard to learners' needs, then how they *are* as people matters. The qualities of empathy, warmth and genuineness which were discussed in Chapters 2 and 3 are important, and it is necessary to be able to convey them to group members. For example, at times it may be helpful to concentrate on being concrete, and learners may need encouragement to talk in specific terms rather than in vague generalities about personal problems they may be having with content and with the learning process; sometimes it may seem important to confront learners about inconsistencies in their thoughts and feelings and this needs to be done tactfully; on occasion it can be constructive to use self-disclosure, and to share personal thoughts, and feelings as a way of helping others to do the same (for further explanation of these terms see, for example, Carkhuff (1969), vols 1 and 2; and Murgatroyd (1985)).

Some tutors, however, may feel there is a risk in actively using the self as a whole person to aid communication. As Knowles (1975, p. 33) has pointed out: 'I divest myself of the protective shield of myself as an authority figure and expose myself as me — an authentic human being'. It is also possible to use the self in a negative way, and to put personal needs before those of the learners. For example, a common way of coping with personal difficulties which people may use without fully realizing what they are doing is to criticize in others unwanted characteristics in the self; or perhaps a need to be at the centre of attention may get in the way of facilitating the learning of others. It is important for tutors, as it is for counsellors, to seek to be aware of personal aims, values, needs and purposes which lie behind their orientation towards this occupation, and to try to use them constructively and not to the detriment of others.

It can be useful, and perhaps necessary, for tutors to reflect at times, either individually or with other tutors, on pitfalls which may arise in the course of teaching, and also to take time to appraise their own performance with regard to the various dimensions of the teaching process. Are they attending to the needs of learners as individuals? Are they aware of group processes and seeking to make the most of group potential? Is information being handled in a variety of ways? Are there personal qualities which might be developed, and different strategies and tactics which might be used? It may be useful perhaps to use self-assessment sheets (see, for example, Mill 1982). In discussion groups and workshops various problems can be explored and ideas and suggestions exchanged (Abercrombie and Terry 1978; Jaques 1984). Tutors have responsibility for academic standards and for themselves as professionals and as individual people. There is no one best way in which to teach any more than there is one best way in which to learn. Each tutor works out his or her own way forward.

INFLUENCES ON THE TEACHING PROCESS

Tutors, like learners, have to cope with internal and external influences on their work. These may act as supports or constraints. If they act as supports, then the task is to make the most of their influence; if as constraints, then the focus of attention is on overcoming or limiting their influence, or adapting to them if no other way if possible.

If tutors accept responsibilities for academic standards and themselves as professionals and as individuals, then it follows that they are also learners, learners who seek to increase their understanding of subject matter and skills, and of other people and of themselves. It may be that from time to time this requires them, as it does any other learner, to move towards a new relationship with the self. This process may involve disturbing internal filing systems, giving up deeply held beliefs, or customary ways of acting, and working through the experience of loss of the familiar and incorporating into the self that which is unfamiliar. It is somewhat difficult to see how a tutor can help others to do this unless he or she knows what it is to work through the process on a personal basis.

External influences on tutors have their origins in immediate settings and in the wider milieu. Those in immediate settings include the characteristics which those whom they teach bring to their study as individuals and as a group. Learners have many different types of resources and of problems, as the discussion on learning has indicated. It may be convenient on occasion to separate out and give special attention to some learners. Perhaps a tutor does not always have the time, or feel sufficiently confident or skilled to help them through some of their difficulties. Some educational institutions provide a source of additional help, particularly with study skills and personal problems. For example, in the Open University all students are allocated to a counsellor to whom they can turn for help; in an increasing number of conventional universities, polytechnics and colleges of further education there is a counselling service available. It is to be regretted that in some institutions counselling services are regarded as entirely separate from academic services, whereas the two are intimately interconnected parts of the process of offering to learners opportunities for self-development.

Some external influences tutors share with their students; such constraints as inconvenient classrooms, and departmental and institutional regulations may be among them. These can affect the teaching process in a variety of ways. It is difficult, for instance, for a large class to subdivide and work in small groups when the seating is fixed permanently in rows. In addition, home life, cultural milieu and the wider conditions of society may support or constrain tutors in their work, as they can learners in their tasks.

STYLES OF TEACHING

It has been suggested that tutors have their own personal orientations towards teaching as an occupation, and that there is no one best way in which to approach the teaching process, or to cope with influences which come to bear upon it. Each tutor develops his or her own style. It is nevertheless possible to make some generalizations about ways in which teaching styles may vary according to the relative importance attached to different aspects of this complex process.

The traditional style of teaching can be described as authoritarian. It can be manifested in a variety of ways. For example, there is the tutor whose only method of teaching is to stand in front of a group and talk. The focus of attention is on the transfer of information between tutor and learners. The tutor decides which information is to be regarded as useful knowledge, how it is interpreted, the language in which it is couched, and how it is passed on. No attention is paid to the aims and needs of learners as individuals, even though they are likely to have a variety of educational orientations and different approaches to learning. They interpret the lectures in their own terms, but there is no opportunity for them to examine different interpretations or to sort out misunderstandings during the course of the lecture, nor is any constructive use made of the resources which they bring with them and could employ to help themselves and one another. They have to remain for the most part passive.

Some tutors may involve students more actively in the teaching/learning process while retaining an essentially authoritarian type of approach. A tutor may 'play games' (in the sense in which Berne (1964) uses this term) in which it is rules which are more important than people (Rhys 1981). For example, there is the game of 'ordering them around'. In this the tutor keeps control of the agenda, always making sure that discussion adheres strictly to it, and takes notice only of those learners who make remarks contributing to it; the tutor asks questions, but only those which allow of yes/no answers. This can be speeded up into a game of 'keeping them moving'. The tutor avoids silences, pounces on individuals with questions, asks multiple questions, interrupts speakers, and ignores non-verbal cues. Another game is 'keeping them guessing'. The tutor has an agenda but does not make it explicit; the students have to guess what it is, and they are allowed to do this in the course of discussion as the tutor reinforces only those remarks relevant to it, and asks questions to which the learners must find the 'right' answers, i.e. the answers deemed correct by the tutor. When put in this concentrated manner games may seem rather like caricatures, but, it is suggested, they embody some common strategies.

The activity of learners may well be to play games in response to the tutor's example. For instance, there is 'the tutor will tell us the answers', in which students sit appreciatively at the feet of the expert, perhaps wheedle or flatter him or her, and beg to be given the 'right' answers. Another game is that of 'pleasing teacher' by working hard to guess what the tutor expects rather than concentrating on the subject matter and the learning process. 'Let's be awkward' is a game which can help to relieve tensions, and can take the form of fooling around, asking many trivial questions very earnestly, or constantly professing not to have quite fully grasped the meaning.

Lectures can be a useful way of passing on information, and games can be fun. The point which is being made here is not that they are inherently wrong in themselves but that if they are the only form of teaching used and arbitrarily imposed on learners, then the help tutors are giving to them must inevitably be restricted. Rigidity on the part of the tutor limits the range of responses of the learners, and can become counterproductive if it results in boredom and a decrease in interest and motivation.

These are styles in which power to order structure and content remains firmly in the hands of the tutor. There is little opportunity for 'authentic human beings' to emerge, or for the group to function as a unit. If the learners have difficulties they are left to flounder in them and are not assisted to become more autonomous. The emphasis is on information for its own sake, and it is not looked at as well as a means to lifelong learning.

It has been suggested that trying to do too much for students can also hinder the development of autonomy. Some tutors, for example, develop an image of the caring parent and like to be seen to be giving help and generally acting as a 'tower of strength'. They are constantly offering advice, telling learners what to learn and do, and how and when to do it. It might even become a matter or pride, possibly encouraged by external departmental pressures, that all members of the group should perform well, so the tutor tries to ensure this by giving meticulous guidance. Possibly on occasion this may be one way of helping some learners over an immediate hurdle, such as a particular examination. But if it is the only style used, it is likely to effectively prevent them from seeking to tackle learning more independently. Once the examination, or whatever, is over they are likely to be very much at sea, and wait expectantly for more instructions. It is possible, however, for there to be at times tension between the requirements posed by the long and short term goals of learners. This necessitates versatility on the part of the tutor to find ways of helping them with both (Rhys and Lambert 1983).

Firm leadership need not necessarily mean domination of the learners by the tutor. Some adults, particularly, for instance, if they are returning to learning for the first time or after a gap of many years and feel apprehensive and unsure of themselves, may welcome initial clear guidance and a well defined role to play. The tutor who is alert not only to immediate but also to long-term needs, however, uses his or her power to encourage a desire for autonomy and gradually relaxes the degree of control over structure and content as learners indicate they are ready for this. Learners are given more freedom within structure, if they wish to use it, to define their own objectives and work out means for attaining them, perhaps through discussion and small working groups, and generally to create a sense of self-direction.

A teaching style in which a tutor may appear to take a back seat does not necessarily mean that he or she is in any way abdicating responsibility for facilitating the learning of others. The tutor is there to guide, to act as a resource person and to offer a helping hand whenever necessary. This role also provides a tutor with an opportunity for observation, reflection and diagnosis of individuals and the group as a unit while in action, so that help offered is more likely to be as appropriate as possible. One writer has gone so far as to suggest that the degree of overt leader activity is often in inverse proportion to the extent of student learning (Bramley 1979). This may seem a somewhat strange notion to tutors and students brought up in a culture in which the education system as a whole is inclined to be hierarchical and authoritarian. Yet the abilities to think critically, to be creative, to use initiative, to solve problems, and so on, can only be developed by learners who are operating independently.

This type of teaching style might be termed 'freedom within structure'. The tutor suggests the framework, and there are many from which to choose, but how a session develops is equally in the control of the learners. For example, there is pyramiding in which people are given a topic to think about as individuals, then they discuss it in pairs, then in fours and eights, before reporting back to a plenary session; there is brainstorming in which a group generates ideas on, say, how to solve a particular problem as fast as possible without attempting to evaluate the ideas, then analyses them and focuses on particular solutions; there are buzz groups in which during the course of a lecture students are asked to turn to their neighbours to discuss any difficulties in understanding or to answer a prepared question; sometimes learners are provided with case notes in a particular problem in advance and are expected to come prepared to share their own ideas or solutions as appropriate; there is the possibility of peer tutoring, perhaps in self-directed student groups, or groups where a student who has already studied a course acts as seminar leader. These are just a few examples. There are other ideas and illustrations to be found in the literature, for example, Ruddock (1978), Abercrombie (1979), Bramley (1979), Main (1980), Gibbs (1981), Jacques (1984).

Freedom for the learners also means freedom for the tutor. How a tutor is seen to use that freedom can of itself by offering a model play an important part in the process of facilitating the learning of group members. For example, such tactics as attentive listening, asking open questions, and checking on meaning by reflecting and summarizing may be noticed and followed, and so may the manner in which they are practised and qualities, such as warmth, empathy and genuineness, which are displayed by the tutor in the process. Tutors are, however, human beings and do not necessarily always do and say what is most appropriate in a given situation. Perhaps they misunderstand students, give rise to confusion by asking too many questions, move on too quickly or too slowly from one point to another, pass on a piece of incorrect information, and so on. Showing him or herself willing to recognize and correct mistakes can also be a useful part of the teaching process, for those who want to learn must be willing to risk making mistakes and, when they do make them, be able to pick themselves up and look for ways and means of correcting them and coping better next time.

Attention is drawn at the end of Chapter 2 to two features in particular of the counselling process. One of these is the nature of the working relationship between helper and person being helped, which, it is suggested, is of itself an important ingredient in the helping process. From the remarks in this section on teaching styles it will be evident that it is being proposed that the same holds true in teaching. When the teaching process includes active participation by the learners on their terms then it seems more likely that their needs are going to be met, and it is not only the content of a session which is important but also the nature of interactions between tutor and learners and between learners, and the climate in which they take place.

The second feature of the counselling process referred to at the end of Chapter 2 is its non-directiveness. This is perhaps more difficult to associate with teaching than with counselling, for teaching is so often bound up with syllabuses and methods of assessment, although more independent study courses are now being established. In most courses, however, the content is laid down, whereas in counselling the content is normally supplied by the person seeking help. But within the constraints of the syllabus etc, it is the learner who has to make decisions about his or her own particular path of learning if that learning is going to be of any more than passing value. A tutor can offer a range of suggestions to learners about how they might extend their knowledge and understanding and resources, but in the end it is the learners who have to select for themselves those which are most appropriate for them as individuals. A basic function of the tutor is to encourage the development of this autonomy.

From the knowledge which we have at present about the processes of learning and teaching it would appear that a style of teaching which is essentially a flexible working partnership is the one most appropriate in adult education. The tutor who adopts this style is not able to plan in detail in advance how a session is going to run, but is likely to go prepared with one or more outline frameworks which are capable of modification, or which might even be changed completely in the course of negotiations with the learners. This style of teaching requires a considerably wider range of resources and skills on the part of the tutor than those usually associated with more traditional approaches. This follows inevitably, however, if it is accepted that the processes of learning and teaching in adult education are as complex as has been suggested in this chapter.

CONCLUDING COMMENTS

Neither learning nor teaching are straightforward processes. Sometimes the teaching-learning system is regarded in the rather simple terms of learners obtaining information and answers to problems from experts. Perhaps it is more accurate to regard it as a whole panorama of tasks and thus to draw attention to the many different ways in which adults might improve the way in which they go about learning, and to the more active part that tutors might take in helping learners to learn how to learn (Hounsell 1984).

If there is a flexible partnership, as was suggested in the last section, tutor and learners operate together in a complex system (Entwistle 1981). To it learners bring their own educational orientations and approaches to learning, and the tutor his or her own occupational orientation and teaching styles. The inputs of both are influenced by the nature of the course content, by internal resources and constraints, and by external conditions. Once the system is in operation inputs are combined, and then recombine as feedback is received by the tutor from the learners, and by the learners from the tutor and from one another. Ideally the process involves all group members as whole persons, as thinking, feeling and doing beings.

It is when learners are regarded as whole persons and not merely as passive recipients of knowledge that it becomes clearer how basic principles of helping associated with the process of counselling are also applicable to teaching. Reference has been made in the course of this chapter to, for example, the importance of recognizing the uniqueness of individual paths of learning, and of encouraging the development of autonomy in learners; to the importance of working relationships between tutor and learners and between learners, and of the climate in which they take place; to the need for tutors to possess a range of strategies and tactics and to encourage a range in learners; and to the importance of self-awareness in tutors, which is a quality it is also important to encourage learners to develop. All of these have their relevance also in counselling. In common with counselling, teaching adults is an open-ended process which can never be perfected. For the tutor committed to facilitating the learning of others however, this is likely to be a basic features of its attractiveness. The complexities of the process are a constant source of interesting and stimulating, if at times somewhat difficult, challenges.

PART B
SOME
APPLICATIONS

CHAPTER FIVE

Counselling at a Distance

TYPES OF CONTACT AT A DISTANCE

Two previous chapters of this book have been concerned to articulate the nature of counselling as a process and the aim of this chapter is to use the ideas presented there and apply them, as a case in point, to the subject of teaching and learning at a distance. Some readers may well find the idea of a chapter on distance education a little surprising, but we would suggest that so far as adults are concerned, learning at a distance is a significant and growing aspect of continuing education. On this basis alone, it should not be ignored in a book of this kind. In addition, however, we would suggest that the potential for counselling adults at a distance exists even in situations where there may be considerable face to face contact between students and tutor.

When we talk about contact at a distance between helper and person seeking help to what specifically do we refer? Perhaps you might like to jot down on a piece of paper a list of various possible categories of interaction between tutor and student at a distance. We can think of at least seven, which we have listed below. Perhaps these categories might be thought of as techniques through which a relationship between tutor and student can be developed.

(a) One-way written material, which provides the student with the opportunity for self-diagnostic assessment and action, e.g. material about giving up smoking.
(b) Two-way written materials such as letters or the completion of essays by students followed by comment and advice/guidance from tutors.

(c) Contact via the telephone.

(d) Contact via the mass media.

(e) One-way contact via audio or video tape e.g. self-instructional material about relaxation or preparing for exams.

(f) Two-way contact via audio-tape in which student and tutor interact with each other by means of sending tapes back and forward.

(g) Computer based contact.

In thinking about all these categories, we need to acknowledge the critical importance of the core counselling conditions of empathy, acceptance and genuineness and skills such as active, attending listening discussed in the previous chapters. The fact that helper and person seeking help may not interact face to face, in no way invalidates their criticality to the counselling process, indeed in some ways it makes them even more central.

STUDENT DROP-OUT

Let us reflect for a moment about these seven categories. Imagine that you are tutor to a group of adult part-time students and that one student with whom you have developed an effective, working relationship suddenly stops coming to the class. The situation is of course a little hypothetical and the background is deliberately left vague. Nevertheless, the issue is one which is not unfamiliar to many tutors of adults, nor should it be too difficult to empathize with the situation; that is to say to put yourself into it. Indeed, this is a useful exercise in the practise of empathy. The question in this situation is what do you do about it? Perhaps you could note down your response on a piece of paper.

We can think of a number of options. One is to do nothing, a second is to write to the student, a third is to telephone, a fourth is to make a home visit. The final option may be unreal in that it involves a degree of familiarity which tutor and student do not possess, so let us consider the other three options as the more practical ones. What is involved in each? What purposes do they serve? What potential do they offer?

A decision to pursue a course of study must lie ultimately with the individual student albeit within structural constraints. The idea of accepting responsibility for one's own learning would lose all credibility if this base line were not to be clearly acknowledged. This point applies equally to decisions taken at the beginning of the education process (to start studying) and the end of the educational process (to cease studying). So far as the latter is concerned this may arise because some natural break-off point has been reached, of which the most obvious is that a formal course has reached its conclusion. But it may also arise because a student drops out. This can happen for a myriad of reasons; concern about progress, lack of confidence, a feeling that fellow group members are unfriendly, lack of confidence in the tutor, domestic or personal difficulties. But whatever the reason, the notion that the final decision lies with the student does not mean that there is no potential in the situation for helping the student. Sometimes non-attendance may represent a message to the tutor or to other group members about needing attention. But even if it is not a conscious statement, subconsciously it may reflect emotional needs (some of which are referred to above) possessed by the student.

Sometimes helper interventions in such situations are institution need directed. For example, a student drops out and as a result a class ceases to be economically or pedagogically viable. Contact is then made by letter or telephone with the student to elicit their intentions, not primarily because of a concern with the student, but because of a concern for maintenance of the system profile in terms of classes. In contrast the counselling perspective insists on a student directed or centred approach, in which the primary concern is not the maintenance of the organization but the welfare of the individual student. In this context, the option of doing nothing itself represents a message to the student and possibly a very negative message. It suggests that the helper doesn't care and it leaves the person needing help in the position of coping alone with the feelings generated by drop-out. Of course, we should not perceive drop-out in totally negative terms. There are often good reasons for non-continuation of a course of study. It may well be that a student has been able to reach a realistic assessment of what is a possibility in a given situation and the fact that the assessment is realistic augurs well for that person's ability to make appropriate decisions in the future. Even so, it helps to know that somebody cares and is interested in one's actions. Helpers should also recognize that they are in a powerful position in relation to students and may well represent significant symbols to the latter. This makes the potential benefit to the student of an expression of interest by the tutor even greater.

LETTERS AND TELEPHONE

We are not suggesting that a reflex action by helpers to student drop-out should be to reach for the pen or the telephone. On the contrary, to do so without thinking carefully about what message the student is making and what expectations he or she has from a possible tutor response may just exacerbate the student's situation. For instance, one reason for the non-continuation of study may be the student's negative perception of the helper. If this is the case, then careful consideration needs to be given about the nature of any approach by the helper. Nevertheless, we are saying that drop-out (the example we quoted) offers the opportunity to do some valuable work with the student. At such a moment of transition, the person in need may well be particularly receptive to the idea of exploring his or her motives, expectations, and feelings about education and perhaps wider areas of their lives. To forego such an opportunity would be to ignore the potential contained within it. To act purposefully would involve acknowledging the potential of the situation for facilitating the student's progress and would mean employing counselling skills. Given that some kind of contact is made, the following brief points can be made initially about the respective merits of letter and telephone. The latter has the advantage of being more immediate in a here and now sense, and interactive. However, the reciprocal of immediacy is that the student is put on the spot. There isn't time to reflect on a response. In contrast, letter writing allows time for reflectiveness by both parties but lacks the qualities of immediacy and spontaneity as well as being less flexibly interactive. It also contains the potential for misunderstanding because of the way language is used. It is of little value to suggest that one is always better than the other. One offers the potential for immediacy/spontaneity, the other for reflectiveness. Being a counsellor involves the helper in weighing up the benefits and losses of different forms of action.

We shall return shortly to looking at the various potentialities for counselling inherent in different kinds of contact at a distance with students. We hope, however, that we have done enough so far to encourage you to think about counselling in situations which are not interactive in a face to face sense. Let us now, therefore, look in more detail at some of the seven categories previously outlined. Our intention is not to explore them all exhaustively, but to set out for your consideration the major issues involved in counselling at a distance.

ONE-WAY WRITTEN MATERIAL
(BIBLIOTHERAPY)

A great deal of educational material is concerned with what we describe as 'bibliotherapy'. In its broadest sense this can refer to the use of any form of literary material, including fiction, in the treatment of physical or physchological problems. However, more recently the term has come to be used more specifically to describe self-help learning, treatment or action programmes that attempt to engage readers in a discussion about personal change. Areas of interest covered by such manuals include hardy perennials like giving up smoking, reducing weight, and feeling less anxious about study skills or exam taking, as well as newer interests in such subjects as reducing drug dependency, getting on better with one's adolescent children, dealing with sexual dysfunctions, feeling more confident sexually, and being more generally assertive in one's day to day interactions. A great deal of continuing education takes place in this way outside formal institutional contexts, through a text which attempts to engage the reader in a learning dialogue in such a way as to promote personal change. Characteristically such materials will offer a large amount of self assessment and diagnostic material, which enables the reader to generate a self-profile and leading through an examination of behaviour and feelings to a plan for action.

Such materials often seek to engage the reader at a variety of levels, including thinking, feeling and behaviour. An example is the Health Education Council's publication on how to stop smoking 'The Smokers Guide to Non-Smoking' (Health Education Council 1984). At the level of thinking, the reader is encouraged to reflect on the patho-logical effects of smoking, but also to think positively about the benefits of non-smoking. Specific images are presented. A plan of action is offered to readers involving a close, even minute examination of the behaviour in question and they are encouraged to relate the behaviour to the expression of particular emotional needs and feelings. The action plan involves the completion of a daily record in which the reader is encouraged to explore his or her feelings relating to the need for cigarettes and the loss involved in giving it up. The attention to all aspects of self, thinking, feeling and behaviour indicates the importance attached to the whole person. The approach generally might be described as eclectic.

We intend this account to focus on the multi-faceted nature of much bibliotherapy material. This fits in well with our humanistic perception of the person as a whole person, not just as a series of parts. However, we should acknowledge that some forms of bibliotherapy are much purer in their approach and focus specifically upon a particular approach to change. Thus there are examples of approaches to change whose principles derive from rational-emotive therapy, transactional analysis, gestalt and behaviourist perspectives, to name but a few of the better known ones. For a contemporary discussion of these perspectives in a British context, we would recommend a book entitled *Individual Therapy in Britain* (Dryden 1984). Of all these specialized approaches, however, the one which has been most influential is that of behaviourism and on this account alone, it merits some special attention.

THE BEHAVIOURIST PERSPECTIVE

The underlying assumption of behaviourism is that people have *learned* to behave in particular ways because that behaviour has, knowingly or unknowingly, been reinforced or rewarded. If old behaviour is learned in this way it follows that it can if so desired, be unlearned and replaced with new, desired behaviour. This proposition offers a direct challenge to the old proposition that the way to amend behaviour is to change attitudes. The equation under behaviourism is reversed; it now reads that if one changes behaviour through learning new patterns of reinforcement, different attitudes will follow from this. An extreme behaviourist approach would argue that internal emotional states as represented by feelings are unmeasurable and, therefore, not worth a lot of time and energy in trying to understand. More flexible behaviourist approaches, however, would acknowledge the role of feelings if only so that an individual can assess and understand such issues as the rewards derived from having a cigarette or eating a chocolate bar. But whereas humanistic approaches would focus on questions about *why* these are rewards, the emphasis of the behaviourist is not on why but on *how* to substitute new rewards for new forms of behaviour. So forexample, the new behaviour of not smoking a cigarette may be reinforced by giving oneself positive strokes for being in control of oneself. All the angst about emotional need is simply side-stepped.

Inevitably, this is a highly simplified account of some sophisticated processes. However, for the reader who is interested in behaviourist approaches through bibliotherapy, there is a detailed account to which we would refer you by Glasgow and Rosen (1978). In their article the authors review the status of self-help behavioural treatment (learning) manuals on programmes for the treatment of phobias, smoking, obesity, sexual dysfunction, assertiveness, child behaviour problems, study skills and physical fitness. They define a behavioural approach as referring to 'modelling, aversive conditioning, desentitization, or operant techniques'. They distinguish between situations in which the person seeking help has no contact at all with the helper, those in which there is minimal contact (perhaps by phone or letter) and those in which contact is strong. In the latter case, meetings may even be centred around the self-help material. There is also discussion about the respective merits of single- and multi-component approaches to treatment. For example, in the case of smoking, research suggests that the former are more effective. They describe a typical multi-component programme as including 'self-monitoring, stimulus control, self-rewards . . . and some types of aversive conditioning [like] . . . rapid smoking'. Perhaps inevitably they conclude that more work remains to be done about the type of programme which works with particular persons under particular conditions.

Of course, the effectiveness of any change involves the question of the extent to which the change is lasting. Many of us, for example, have had the experience of managing to eat, smoke or drink less for a period of time and yet of finding it difficult or impossible to maintain the change in the long term. Quite simply we slip back into old habits. Behaviourists would argue that this represents the result of a treatment programme which was inadequate. It is very much to their credit that they are prepared to acknowledge such deficiencies in their own learning programmes instead of suggesting that the person is unsuitable for the treatment which is the usual response to a failed learning programme. However, our view is that the behaviourist position greatly oversimplifies the character of human beings. Our contention is that the potential for lasting change is limited unless we understand why we behave in the ways we do and what emotional needs are served for us by such behaviour — all questions largely ruled out of court by the behaviourist approach. Such approaches emphasize self-awareness as a prerequisite for personal change. Moreover, change is seen as involving feelings and thought processes as well as behaviour. In other words, we are back with the notion of the whole person. It seems to us, therefore, that if bibliotherapy is to achieve its objectives, some way has to be found, through the text, of addressing the whole being; the bit of the person that is emotional, concerned with hopes, fears and anxiety as well as the bit that is rational and logical and employs thinking processes.

Jacques (1984) refers to this as 'habeas emotum'. He puts it this way.

> Many of the above issues may seem far-fetched to academic tutors, especially those in the physical sciences and engineering whose central concern is not with personal feelings and group process but with the imparting of a body of knowledge. Yet, with these faculty areas one hears of constant problems to do with lack of motivation and commitment, alienation and even drop-out. . . . Behaviour is determined as much by passions, anxieties and convictions as it is by reason, the more so when we are not aware of the effects of our feelings.

Learning involves a complex process of assimilating new material with what we already possess. In this way the learner can be said to be transformed as a person. The mere fact of engaging in a process of learning itself changes us, irrespective of the content with which that learning is concerned. But of course change is not something which is always readily accepted. It is challenging, even threatening to our perception of ourselves and the ways in which we see the world. Indeed, it often produces a lot of resistance. This is particularly the case when we are exposed to ideas which we do not like. Imagine for a moment a time when you attended a lecture; with whose content you disagreed. Now ask yourself how you *felt* on this occasion? Many people would say that they felt threatened or attacked by what they were asked to learn and felt angry with the lecturer for presenting such ideas. Our point is that you felt emotions such as these; your emotions entered into the learning process.

If this is the case with a lecture on science or economics or literature, subjects which on the face of it seem to be objective and emotionally neutral, how much more true this must be if one is engaging students with written material in such emotionally charged areas as trying to stop smoking, reduce weight, get on better in one's personal relationships, or examine one's anxieties about taking examinations or generally feeling less than fully competent in coping with a programme of formal study. Each subject area has particular teaching problems of its own, but unless the writer is adopting a highly mechanical behavioural approach, each will involve the writer in ensuring that the student is confronted with a number of questions about feeling saturated areas, relating to:

(a) motivation for wanting to study the subject;
(b) expectations about what studying the subject might produce in terms of changes in feeling, thinking, bodily states and behaviour;
(c) emotional needs met by particular types of behaviour;
(d) problems posed for the individual by trying to change;
(e) previous experience of learning in the particular area in question and feelings about it.

It is useful at this stage to think about the process involved in devising a written package which will be both confrontative and yet supportive to the person seeking help. The first component of such a package is to help the latter to make an exact assessment or diagnosis of his or her starting position in terms of feelings, attitudes and behaviour. Having worked towards a self-assessment, the student may need help in clarifying objectives; where he or she wants to get to, as opposed to where they are now. Sometimes individuals are clear about this, but some, even many, may need help in breaking down broad aims into a series of smaller and achievable objectives. Throughout this process the person seeking help can be encouraged to look at what their needs are and examine different options for satisfying these needs. Thirdly, having helped the individual to define (a) where he or she begins from and (b) where they want to get to, the student has also to be helped to devise a programme which will see him or her through from (a) to (b). This may involve the development of skills in areas such as planning, negotiating, decision making and assertiveness. It may also involve looking at obstacles, both internal and external, to the desired change. Finally, it may necessitate providing the student with some form of training in evaluation so that he or she can be clear about whether the desired goal or objective has been achieved. Sometimes this is straightforward, as in the case of a programme of learning concerned with stopping smoking. It may be less clear, however, in other more diffuse areas such as developing more satisfactory personal relationships or to become less indecisive. Throughout this whole process, one of the key forms of pedagogy lies in encouraging the student to draw up a realistic personal contract or contracts for himself or herself and encouraging and supporting them to stick with the terms of what they have devised for themselves as a realistic programme.

DIETING

At this point we would like to offer a few examples of the process we have outlined. Dieting is one subject on which many people spend a great deal of time and energy. In 'The Good Health Guide' produced by The Open University in collaboration with the Health Education Council and the Scottish Health Education Unit (Open University *et al*. 1980), this problem is addressed in the following way (our paraphrasing):

(a) Readers are asked to work out how much they should weigh. This provides the person seeking help with an objective to work towards as well as a statement about their base position; where they are in relation to this objective.

(b) The negative aspects of overweight are pointed out. This is done not just in logical effect on body image and social relationships. Being fat we are told 'can make you lonely! Some people do seem to be "fat and jolly" but other seemingly "jolly fatties" are just playing the clown. They make fun at themselves rather than wait for someone else to do it. But it hurts inside.' One might describe this account as encouraging the reader to confront negative feelings which he or she possesses and to accept or own these feelings; to accept responsibility for one's own overweightness. The term 'fat' or 'fat person' is used consistently. It feels more powerful than the more emotionally neutral 'overweight'.

(c) An account is offered of how people have learned poor patterns of eating. Readers are encouraged to relate reasons to their own experience. In this way, they gain a better grasp of the reason why they are overweight.

(d) Attention is focused on an action programme for reducing food intake. The emphasis is on educating students into learning new ways of behaving in respect of food.

STUDY SKILLS

We have tried in this above account to pick up the essential features of how a text attempts to engage students in a debate about the subject of over eating. Throughout, students are seen as active learners and the barriers to change are confronted and explored. The person seeking help is perceived as a whole person, not just a brain but a complex ever-interacting mixture of body, mind and emotions. Another example of the genre is the course produced by the National Extension College on the skills of studying (Sullivan 1979). At one level the student is offered an account of the skills involved in studying such as reading, note taking, writing essays and tackling examinations. By breaking these skills down into their component parts, students are encouraged to practice them in a series of exercises, so that they are better able to apply them in real life. But the course is about more than just the behaviour of learning new skills. It is also concerned with encouraging students to explore their own feelings of learning competence, to come to terms with their own feelings of anxiety, to acknowledge their motivation and the effect this has on the learning methods they adopt. The person to be helped, the reader, is addressed as an adult with likely family commitments which may have an effect on and be influenced by the experience of being a student. Overall the message is that study skills are more than just a matter of technique but are also a function of self-awareness. The thrust of the text is to engage the person seeking help in a process of self-discovery through which he or she can better understand their feelings and motives as learner and through this greater understanding come to see the relevance and applicability of certain skills. The point is that the skills are not mechanical ones. Their effective practice and the success of the course as bibliotherapy, depends on the student moving down the road of self-awareness and discovery.

Bibliotherapy, therefore, involves the employment of written material to produce change in the reader in such a way that will enable or facilitate the person seeking help to make the changes which he or she desires. To be successful it has to take account of a learner's emotional needs and responses to the written word and the changes this generates in the individual. Somehow it has to engage with the student in a process of counselling at a distance. Other examples of this process in action are to be found in the Open University's First Year Student Handbook (Open University 1985) or 'The Good Health Guide' (op.cit. 1980) which contains chapters on anxiety, sex, smoking, dieting, and others.

COUNSELLING VIA THE TELEPHONE

A great deal of contact between tutor and student takes place through the medium of the telephone. We have already referred to the issue of responding to student drop-out by telephone contact. But of course this is just the tip of the iceberg. Learners themselves often contact their tutors in this way to talk not just about the content of their learning, but also about their fears and anxieties. At a more institutional level, the widespread development of adult information, guidance and counselling centres (which we discuss in detail in the next chapter) depends heavily on the telephone for contact with students. Our experience is that many persons who seek advice need help in developing a diffuse expression of interest into a more concrete and practical proposal. So for example a person telephones an advisory service with a query about whether there are any interesting courses on offer in the area. Discussion over the telephone reveals that the enquirer is a married woman in her late thirties whose children are all now full-time at school, and who is working through a transitional period of change in her life, part of which concerns present and future vocational directions. Discussion over the telephone (a) establishes the basis of a working relationship, however brief, between advisor and student and (b) assists the person seeking help to begin the process of clarifying her objectives. It may be that the single telephone call is all that is necessary in helping the enquirer to focus on perhaps a particular course or line of study. It may be that the telephone call is followed by a visit from the student. It may be that the call is just the starting point, or a marker point along a longer road, for further enquiries. But in each situation, the advisor is better able to help if he or she is able to consider the student's needs in the round (as a whole) and to employ counselling skills of *empathy* (trying to understand what it felt like to be that other person: get inside their world); *acceptance* (accepting them for what they are, warts and all, even if their values are different from your values); *honesty* (being aware of one's own feelings; not for example dismissing a person because their lack of ambition makes you feel angry); and *concreteness* (being specific and avoiding vagueness). The fact that the person seeking help is at a distance makes the use of these skills all the more necessary if the advisor is to engage in anything other than a superficial interaction with the caller.

The example above illustrates a case in which the enquirer

presents a rather diffuse request which the advisor helps to develop into a more concrete proposal. But of course the process of helping contains an infinite variety of circumstances. For example, sometimes the exact opposite can happen to the case desribed above. A caller, for instance, says he wants to know how to become a teacher. Through forming a working relationship with him, the advisor discovers that he is a man in his late forties who is dissatisfied with his present career and wishes to change direction. The choice of teaching is less an expression of desire to move into that field than of his wish to change the present course of his life. Through careful listening and a display of empathy, the advisor helps him to see that the most constructive way forward is to use education as a vehicle for getting to know himself a little better. In this case, therefore, a specific request is changed into a more open-ended educational search.

Beyond the use of telephones in advisory and counselling services, there is considerable experience now available of the use of telephones in formal teaching. The Open University, for example, employs the idea of a loudspeaking conference call network to link together tutor and students who may be widely scattered geographically. In some cases, in courses with low populations, telephone tuition may be the only form of contact between students and tutor. However, in the Open University formal telephone tuition is regarded as a back-up to face to face teaching. In other countries a different priority applies. For example, in the well-known Wisconsin University Educational Telephone Network (see Moore 1981), a private telephone link is employed as the main form of contact between student and tutor. Correspondence material (unlike the Open University) is reduced to a supporting role and face to face contact (again unlike the Open University) is virtually non-existent. Moore stresses the highly interactive nature of telephone tuition. At the same time this has to be reconciled with a need for structure. Typically it helps to have an agenda or at least some prior agreement about topics to be discussed and the way time is to be used. It follows, therefore, that a balance has to be struck between on the one hand the potential for spontaneity offered by the telephone and on the other hand the need to provide some forum of agreed structure if the spontaneity is not to degenerate into chaos. In other words, spontaneity cannot be open-ended. As Moore puts it 'while permitting both teachers and learners to interrupt a presentation, or to follow unplanned and unexpected lines of enquiry and discussion, the whole has to be contained within well-determined boundaries'.

Particularly where face to face contact is limited or non-existent, the use of the telephone as a counselling vehicle becomes an important aspect of the helper's task. The group on the telephone may be as important as the face to face group in providing a safe forum in which mutual problems can be aired and shared; problems concerning anxieties over study skills or fear of failure being particularly important in this context. Where contact is individual to individual, the range of personal issues raised by students may be wider. But in all cases exposure of intimate aspects of self will depend on the establishment of an effective working alliance between tutor and student, in which the latter feels that the former can be trusted and the former is aware of the latter as a person with feelings as well as an intellect.

One critical way in which telephone contact differs from face to face communication places special demands on the tutor as counsellor (see George 1983). We refer to the lack of visual contact and the premium this puts on the importance of checking out the student's understanding and interest. As George puts it, 'there's a silence — and I don't know whether they're deep in thought, quite baffled — or just asleep. Unless they say, it's difficult to tell what they need . . . it is far easier for misunderstandings to arise.'

This quotation is taken from a package produced by the Open University specifically about counselling and teaching by telephone. The text explores how skills of teaching such as information giving, checking out understandings, offering advice, negotiating, providing feedback and so on, can be adapted for use in a non-visual medium. Included in the package is an audio-cassette containing a range of examples. One conclusion which emerges clearly from this package is for there to be a clear agenda and structure to telephone sessions, particularly group sessions. The helper, therefore, has to act as a manager of the situation and to adopt a relatively directive role, at least in planning a link-up. While this particular package includes counselling in its title, it should be made clear that it is not about crisis counselling, but is aimed specifically at those using the telephone in an educational context.

Nevertheless, a great deal of crisis counselling is done through the telephone. While the Samaritans choose not to describe themselves as counsellors, preferring the term 'befrienders' the agency is well-known and respected for its work in the field, particularly its concern with assisting callers who feel suicidal. Accounts of the practice of helpers emphasise the importance of listening and caring (Chad Varah 1985). But of course people seek help via the telephone for reasons other than concern over suicidal feelings. Other organizations concerned with offering help include Family Network, Niteline (for higher education students) and Rape Crisis centres. In an interesting study of local services in the West Midlands, Davies (1982) investigated the quality of services offered by telephoning ten different hotlines with a role-played problem. This concerned pressure felt by a client from his family who wished him to get married. After considering a large variety of responses which he received, Davies concluded that

> agencies tend to over-promote their services: those offering counselling on a limited range of subjects only should say so in their publicity. In addition, more attention is needed to the quality of the help that is offered. The client's expectations were to have an interested and sympathetic person to listen to, so that he could ventilate his feelings. No great amount of professionalism and experience were needed for this. Yet far too many of the counsellors thought that they had to give advice. Furthermore, by not listening carefully enough, several fell into the trap of proffering totally inappropriate advice.

While educational guidance services (discussed in more detail in the next chapter are not the same thing as hotline agencies) there are some parallels with the latter and messages which can be learned. In particular, there is often a degree of confusion in educational guidance services relating to whether their primary concern is with filling places on courses at the institution which offers advice or with offering a more dispassionate, student centred service. This might involve telling students that they would do better elsewhere at another institution or that such and such a course is not suitable for them. We should also avoid complacency about the quality of the services offered. A great deal of enquiry work is handled by untrained clerical and secretarial staff who happen to operate the telephone switchboard. They answer some queries directly and channel others as they see appropriate. In many ways they can be described as the gatekeeper of the educational process. There is a need in this area for training which will ensure that enquirers will receive better service. This should also benefit those people working at the switchboards in the sense of enhancing job satisfaction.

We do not have the space to log each and every example of the use of the telephone as a vehicle for helping. But the number of possible uses is large and growing. An example from a slightly different field is the Healthline experiment in the East End of London. Established by the College of Health, it is designed to help people unable to approach their doctors with problems considered to be too trivial or embarrassing. By dialling a local telephone number, callers can request the playback of more than 200 tape cassettes which give detailed advice on all kinds of medical problems. The use of tape cassettes is equivalent to the use of simple home computers in the sense that there is no possibility of a developing interaction between helper and person seeking help, though a new generation of computer software is being developed which is beginning to address this problem. The telephone, however, already offers this quality of immediacy and interaction and it is this quality which we have illuminated in this discussion. So far as the helper is concerned, all the principles of counselling are of vital importance in ensuring that the potential of the medium is maximized. So checking out is crucial, just as it is crucial in counselling, not just so that the helper is sure that he or she understands what the other person is saying, but because it is necessary to demonstrate this understanding back to the other person; to show them that you have really heard, really understood what they have tried to communicate to you.

TAPE CASSETTES

The Healthline experiment illustrates the use of tape recorders, but there are many other examples. A number of relaxation tapes are now widely available on the open market, some concerned generally with helping listeners to cope with stress, some concerned with more specific issues such as coping with examination nerves and anxiety. So far as the latter is concerned, even within the particular context of the Open University there are to be found examples both of tapes sent to students through the post and also of the provision of a recorded tape which students can listen to by dialling a telephone number. The two forms of receiving a message by cassette are not quite analogous. So far as the telephone is concerned, it has the advantage as we have already seen of immediacy. If you want the information, you dial the number, any time of day or night. However, the tape through the post, while it may take time to be received, has the useful facility of a stop-start button. This gives students a greater degree of control and allows for as much repetition as required. It also enables the learner to study the message at a pace suitable to each individual and gives the opportunity for reflection and analysis. Compared with the printed word, a cassette is much more personal and informal, a factor which may be very significant in sensitive areas like coping with anxiety or fear of failure. A number of tutors in the Open University for example, have found a recorded tape message useful in helping students to cope with the feelings engendered by the receipt of a disappointingly low grade.

In all these ways, the audio cassette represents a cheap and perhaps surprisingly personalized way of bridging the distance gap between helper and person seeking help. But it contains another important asset, namely that it allows for interaction with print or other visual material. In this way it can function as a key linking medium in a multi-media package. A successful example of this approach, particularly pertinent in this discussion, is the BBC radio series on 'Principles of Counselling' (BBC 1978 and 1983) which used tape in conjunction with open circuit broadcasts and a printed booklet in order to teach counselling skills. Bates (1982) has suggested that the extra control brought to students by audio material is also possible in theory for television.

While this account is relatively brief, we hope it demonstrates the potential of cassettes for helping, not just in a tutoring function but also in a counselling role. This involves helping the student to better understand the processes, both mental and emotional through which learning is mediated.

ADVICE AND COUNSELLING THROUGH RADIO AND TELEVISION

The role of broadcasting as an educational medium is not in doubt. The Charter of the BBC declares that its function is 'information, education and entertainment' and both the BBC and ITA employ full-time Education Officers. While for many adults radio and television has represented their major educational vehicle, Legge (1982) suggests that increasingly the main educational contribution of broadcasting will be as 'a partner in the learning process, one of several agencies helping the adult'. Another new partnership represented by the increasing interest of people working in broadcasting is with the field of advice and counselling. It may well be that most readers of this book will not be professional broadcasters and that at first sight the combination of broadcasting and counselling may seem of little interest to this majority; a topic best left to Clare Raynor — or so it may seem. However, we think that the advent of local radio raises some interesting options for a large number of persons involved in the continuing education of adults and it is in this light that we proceed with this discussion.

In an unpublished paper, Paterson and Blashko (1984) discuss their experience of running an advice column on local radio in Edmonton, Canada. They stress that the choice of topics, number of calls accepted and recommendations provided were all decisions made by the professional advisors rather than the broadcasters. Topics raised over 176 programmes included such education related issues as 'People Using People', 'Talking Straight', 'Controlling our Emotions', 'Why we develop Anxiety and Panic Attacks', 'Relaxation', 'Basic Problems in Basic Education', 'Trouble with Specialization', 'School-yard Violence', 'Learning by Doing', 'Psychological Testing', and 'Study Habits'. Listeners are perceived as advice givers as well as receivers. The authors suggest widespread approval, both from listeners and from professional bodies about their work. Nevertheless a number of questions must be asked about the ethics and standards of such use of broadcasts and in 1984 a conference was convened of interested parties out of which a paper was produced entitled 'Advice and Counselling through the Broadcast Media in the United Kingdom' (BAC *et al.* 1984).

The paper suggests that the broadcasting media have a number of advantages as advice givers over other sources of help. These include:

(a) the perceived intimacy of advice received in the home;
(b) education through hearing about other people's problems;
(c) learning about sources of help.

The document proceeds to set out a list of seventeen guidelines for advice and counselling through the broadcast media, of which perhaps the most important are:

(a) a clear understanding of whether the aim of a programme is to provide advice, referral or counselling;
(b) awareness of such problems and how to avoid them as sensationalism, unwarrented invasion of privacy, false

identification with another person's problems, misunderstandings due to brevity and time constraints and the need
to generalize from specific enquiries to the detriment of the
individual enquirer;
(c) need for an off-air back-up service and communication of its
nature to listeners e.g. leaflet or personal advice;
(d) adequate back-up resources like telephone and leaflets;
(e) callers not dealt with on a programme should be dealt with
either by referral or directly off-air.

Both the BBC and ITA assert their support to the guidelines 'as a basis
for developing a high standard of advice and counselling through the
broadcast media'.

Nevertheless we need to avoid complacency. One of the speakers
at the conference referred to above, has rightly pointed out (Hawkins
1985) that 'helping is not just a matter of goodwill'. In fact she goes
further and argues 'that you simply cannot counsel or indeed advise
on radio and television. As far as I can see for real advice and counselling you need time, you need the freedom to travel up a variety of
blind alleys, the client should be free to be devious in their approach
to their own problem, he or she has to be the focus of the exchange,
and whatever the helper says must be felt to be absolutely specific to
the person in need of help. None of these rules holds true of a live
broadcast.' What a skilled counsellor can do is to offer personal
encouragement and support and some broad guidelines so that the
audience learns a bit more about life and may have found something
of specific relevance to their own lifes. A similar point of view is
expressed by the editor of the 'problem page' in the magazine
Woman, (Willans 1984). As she puts it 'a middle-aged man rings up a
radio phone-in programme and talks about his suicidal thoughts. The
"media person" responds sympathetically but briskly, touches lightly
on what causes him to feel that way, suggests some sources of help
and eases him off the air to make room for the next caller.' Is this, she
asks, really counselling? She answers her question by suggesting that
if we define counselling as helping a client to listen to him or herself,
based on an understanding of the real need and situation of the individual seeking help, it would be hard to define the standard one-off
media contact as such.

Paterson and Blasko (1986) however, have specifically challenged
the views put forward by Hawkins. They point out that media counselling is now well known in the USA and that while there are

dangers, 'these are outweighed many many times by the advantages'. In their view these include the following:

(a) If advice is to be given, it is best for this to be provided by competent and qualified professionals. To reject all advice giving because some of it is of poor quality is not an argument for stopping offering help but rather in favour of qualified persons becoming involved. Not to do so runs the risk of throwing out the baby with the bathwater. Moreover, referrals to traditional agencies increase when they are mentioned 'on air'.

(b) The widespread belief that to be interesting, advice givers must be dynamic or controversial or talkers rather than listeners is quite erroneous. What media counselling does is to educate the public — with regards to the facilities and services available to them. 'One of the main things we are doing is reinforcement — getting people to know the kind of professional they need for a particular problem' (Oglov 1984).

(c) There is an enormous potential for preventive work with the public in fields such as preventing coronary problems and smoking.

While to some extent the views of Hawkins and Paterson and Blashko are diametrically opposed — indeed the latter is a specific riposte to the former — we need to acknowledge that in Britain this is still a new and expanding field. Values and boundaries are being defined, as it were 'on the hoof'. In such a context, we would perhaps do well to heed the advice given to helpers by Willans which essentially is not to be too purist. There are many agencies which purport to offer counselling yet which in practice cannot be said to be value neutral. For example, agencies concerned with abortion (whether facilitating or hindering it) represent one example. The key question, therefore, is perhaps not whether an agency describes itself as offering a counselling service, but whether its concern is to say to the client 'hear yourself', or 'hear me'. Any helper who is expressing the former philosophy can be said, at the very least, to have his or her work informed by a counselling approach.

It is in this spirit, given that counselling on radio and television is now a reality, that we suggest that there is a great opportunity here for persons involved in adult and continuing education to use local radio particularly in the area of offering advice to potential students.

As experience grows in this area, it is important for knowledge to be shared and codified, so that the most appropriate procedures can be encouraged and developed within a framework of closely defined ethical and moral standards.

SUMMARY

This chapter has been concerned to demonstrate the potential for counselling at a distance. This is now a clearly established and recognized form of education for adults and it is hardly speculative to suggest that it is likely to remain so. Indeed, the chances are that as the idea of education as a continuing or recurrent theme in a person's life replaces the old notion of education as a terminal apprenticeship for a working life, distance education will continue to grow in importance. If this is the case, workers in the field will be forced even more to consider the need for, provision of and impact of counselling at a distance. Developments in the field of information technology simply extend the possibilities even beyond those we have discussed in this chapter. A recent edition of the *British Journal of Guidance and Counselling* is devoted almost entirely to the theme of 'Counselling and Computers' (see Sugarman 1986). That symposium provides a framework within which helpers can examine the role of computers in relation to their work and we explore this subject ourselves in Chapter 7 of this book. We hope that this chapter on counselling at a distance has made a contribution towards disseminating information and increasing knowledge and awareness of the potential of distance education for helpers and helping in adult and continuing education.

CHAPTER SIX

Educational Guidance Services

INTRODUCTION — THE VARIETY OF PROVISION

In this chapter our intention is to explore the nature of educational guidance services for adults. While there have been some interesting experiments in this field during the 1970s and 80s, the provision seems to have 'grown like topsy'. Legge (1982) suggests that 'even the most common type of provision, that of supplying information about adult opportunities for education, is uncoordinated and often bewildering to potential students'. Services from which adults can get information include the institutions actually offering courses, local LEA offices, local libraries, the Citizens Advice Bureaux, Manpower Services Commission (local job centres), professional associations, and local information and advisory services. This list is by no means exhaustive. However, the provision of local guidance services is a relatively new provision. Butler (1983) has suggested that the 1970s witnessed a number of kinds of changes which are outlined below.

EXPANSION IN THE 1970s

First an expansion in the provision of vocational guidance for adults was experienced. The Education and Training Act of 1973 empowered local authority careers services to extend their guidance and placement services to adults. The same act also established the Manpower Services Commission which also involved itself in the provision of vocational guidance through such avenues as its occupational Guidance Unit, TOPS (Training Opportunity Scheme) — which highlighted the need for presenting advice — and WOW (Wider Opportunity for Women); scheme which offered work taster experiences and as Butler put it 'again demonstrated the importance of guidance before, during and after attendance'. The importance of these developments should not be underestimated. Watts (1981) has indicated how the term 'career development' was introduced to careers guidance as late as 1957 (see Super 1957). Before that vocational guidance was based on psychological testing which sought to match the qualities of the person with the requirements of the job. While educational guidance is not synonymous with careers guidance, it clearly represents an important aspect of it.

Another development of the 1970s as seen by Butler lay with the growth of the idea of continuing education so as to bring within the aegis of formal education many persons with little previous post-secondary formal education. The Open University is itself a manifestation of this development and its built-in provision of a counselling service for students has been seen as one of its most imaginative experiments. Indeed, the ability of the Open University to avoid a high drop-out particularly in comparison with similar institutions in other Western countries like the Fernuniversitat of West Germany, has been attributed to the local support network of tuition and counselling services it offers to its students (Sewart 1981).

Other developments too, like the Adult Literacy programmes, indicated the need for guidance services for adults and this was reflected in the provision made by the Adult Literacy and Basic Skills Unit (ALBSU) as well as many New Opportunities for Women (NOW) courses. The more that education began to be conceived as a continuing or recurrent element of an adult's life (rather than as a terminal apprenticeship for a working life) the more necessary became the need for guidance for adults returning to learning. These needs related to such things as finding out details about courses, understanding and choosing between the range of options available, and relating personal and vocational needs to educational organization and structures. Butler suggests that 'such considerations indicated the desirability of a collaborative model for the provision of educational guidance', a theme already enunciated some years previously by Murgatroyd and Redmond (1978) who attempt to 'identify different operational constructions of collaboration' with respect to a number of advisory services.

COLLABORATION

Such a task is necessary in order to make some kind of sense of the multiplicity of educational guidance services which developed from the late 1970s onwards. The field is characterized by a variety of terms like 'information', 'advice', 'guidance' and 'counselling', and it is often difficult to draw boundaries between categories and to know where for example advice giving ends and counselling begins. What is the difference, for example, between an Adult Education Information and Survey Project (Sheffield), an Educational Resources and Information Centre (Cardiff), or an Educational Guidance Service for Adults (Belfast)? The last named is the longest running service of this kind in the United Kingdom. Murgatroyd and Redmond (1978) offer a model which emphasizes the question of how far the enterprise results from one institution or body acting unilaterally or conversely the extent to which it is an integrated project. They perceive the balance of advantage as lying with the latter, if only because it is more likely to ensure the continued funding of a project. This is a field in which there is a tremendous amount of wastage, of projects which begin, flower briefly and then die for lack of continued funding. An integrated approach also helps to get away from the insular institution oriented advice of some information providing. In particular the recruitment motive remains powerful, particularly at a time when institutions compete for students as a scarce resource. This means that students receive advice which is not wholly objective or dispassionate, but is related to the need of institutions to recruit students. Integration, however, is a word which is hard to achieve in practice, however good it sounds in theory. For one thing the message provided by integration, namely that there is a need for rationalization of services across providers, is one which is often difficult for providers to accept. Rationalization often results in an overall reduction in the amount of institutional provision and a possible loss of jobs or status for particular institutions. We do not think that this issue is an academic one within the field of continuing education. Indeed it relates to a topic raised in the previous chapter, and highly germane to any discussion of counselling: in whose interests is guidance and counselling perceived, those of the individual or those of the organization? It is only when the interests of the former are given priority that we can refer to the student (client) centred counselling discussed in Chapters 2 and 3.

ADVOCACY

Increasingly, workers in this field have begun to extend the focus of their work so that it includes some consideration of the institutional context in which student and tutor work. Terms like 'advocacy' and 'brokering' are now being used to imply that the tutor in his or her counselling role has a concern not just in working with the student (client) but also with the system, so that it becomes more flexible and adaptive to the needs of clients. In the words of Hefferan *et al*. (1976),

> client advising means placing learners' needs and interests above those of the institution's. This advising for clients' interests takes two forms: intercession on behalf of individual students, and efforts to change individual policies which hamper adult learners' re-entry and progress.

So what is being argued here is a more radical interventionist policy than that usually conceived as encompassed in the role of information provider about education. Agencies like Community Law Centres or Centres for unemployed people represent the most thoroughgoing examples of this more radical form of provision.

The authors of this book have personal knowledge of this area as a result of their involvement in the Educational Resources Information Centre (ERIC) which operated in Cardiff between 1977 and 1979. Essentially what advocacy boils down to is a need to take private problems and ensure their transformation into the public domain, so as to ensure local policy changes. In practice, this involves issues such as knowing what courses are available and how this supply relates to what people actually want, or how the scheduling of courses relates to the life patterns and needs of potential students. Other issues which emerged concerned the question of making it easier for students to take courses in local authorities other than the one in which they were resident and in the provision of courses and other services for which a demand existed yet for which no provision had hitherto been made. The provision of non-recruitment motivated advice services to potential students is yet another area of advocacy.

DIRECTIVE AND NON-DIRECTIVE FORMS OF GIVING HELP

As we have already pointed out, the discussion is particularly relevant to those of us involved with the education of adults because it raises the issue of how far the service we offer is oriented towards meeting the needs of the client or the system. However, another dimension along which we can usefully assess and evaluate guidance services to students is the extent to which they are directive or non-directive in emphasis. The inclusion of the two terms 'guidance' and 'counselling' in the title of this book reflects the meaningfulness of this dimension and the extent to which it is reflected in the practice of educators. The term guidance is the one of longer standing. It impies that when people come to us for help, we give them guidance or advice. When we talk about offering adults an information service it is to this kind of provision that we usually refer. The model of helper-student interaction sees the former in fairly active and the latter in relatively passive terms. The role of the latter is essentially to state what his or her needs are. Moreover, the assumption is that these needs can be articulated more or less straightforwardly in a fairly concrete form. The skills required by the tutor or helper can be described as diagnostic and concerned to reach an outcome in terms of decision making which will resolve the student's enquiry.

In contrast, counselling implies a more non-directive or student (client) centred approach. The person who comes for help is perceived as an active learner and the relationship between tutor and student is seen as one in which the former acts as a facilitator or enabler of learning in the latter. There is no assumption that needs can be readily articulated. Rather, a process is entered into (of which the relationship between tutor and student is a key component) in which the emphasis is less with the outcome of decision making than in helping the student to understand and to come to terms with the process of decision making in which he or she is engaged. A major advantage of this form of learning process is that because the student is actively involved in the processes of decision making he or she has the opportunity to develop learning strategies that can potentially be transferred to other areas of personal development, change or transition in the future.

We think it is worthwhile dwelling on this distinction. Terms like information, advice, guidance and counselling are often used fairly interchangeably, but what we think is important is to be clear about the difference between directive and less directive approaches (we think it best to see it as a continuum rather than as two polarities). It may be that your experience has largely been in one or the other and that you find the other notion rather unfamiliar and disconcerting.

For example to some people counselling can seem rather vague because it often appears somewhat open ended, lacking in structure and moving power away from the tutor onto the student. Conversely guidance can appear narrow in scope, restrictive and shallow. We think that there is a role for both approaches in the education of adults. Our purpose is to extend the range of options, not to foreclose choices. To assist in this task, we have presented below a list of the major differences between the counselling and guidance (advice giving) perspectives (Table 6.1). In the process of examining this table, you may find it useful to ask yourself how it relates to the life concerns and motivations enunciated in the table in Chapter 1. Many persons who do seek advice are facing mid-life issues about feelings of creativity and usefulness.

Table 6.1 SOME BASIC DIFFERENCES BETWEEN COUNSELLING AND GUIDANCE

	Counselling	*Guidance (advice giving)*
(a)	Student-directed. Locus of control moves towards student.	Tutor-directed. Locus of control remains with tutor.
(b)	The tutor is a facilitator/enabler.	The tutor is an information/advice giver.
(c)	Tutor and student jointly negotiate a contract about agenda and methodology.	Tutor determines objectives and methods.
(d)	Student participates with tutors in assessing needs and evaluating progress.	Assessment/diagnosis and evaluation is the domain of the tutor.
(e)	Concern is with the process of decision-	Concern is with making a decision (decision seen as

Table 6.1 *Contd*

	Counselling	Guidance (advice giving)
	making. Understanding how a decision is reached is as important as the content of the decision.	product). The way it is reached is not regarded as especially significant.
(f)	Learning is seen as transferable. What is learned in one context is seen as utilizable in others, e.g. the learning of a skill such as breaking down a problem into its component parts.	Learning is seen as specific to the problem in question.
(g)	Learning is seen as an emotional as well as a cognitive experience.	Feelings are not regarded as important in learning.
(h)	Learning about a subject is seen as involving a process of learning about self.	Learning about a subject is not seen as involving self-discovery.

In considering these lists, in our view an important issue would be the extent to which the counselling mode fosters in the individual a sense of personal responsibility for his or her own learning and decision making. If you think that this is the case, you may well conclude that the sense of commitment to any decision which is reached may be that much stronger.

ASPECTS OF EDUCATIONAL GUIDANCE

While the directive, non-directive distinction or continuum is a crucial one, there are other ways in which we may categorize the service provided in terms of its edcuational process. For example, in a recently published comparison of four Education Guidance services (Butler 1984), the researchers distinguish between four aspects of any service, which they describe as 'advice', 'information', 'assessment' and 'implementation'. Information giving implies the existence of some kind of data base, either in the written form of prospectuses, information sheets or card indexes or through a computer. Most queries in the four services researched were for information, thus indicating the general lack of knowledge of educational and training opportunities by adults. This is hardly surprising. Unlike school-children, adults are often isolated from a network of contacts and communications about education. With regard to assessment, the helper's role is to explore the client's personal biography including educational and vocational history, abilities, potential aspirations and financial circumstances. Interestingly, a need is seen for appropriate psychometric testing, though as we have already indicated it was as a reaction against this procedure that the concept of development began to be used in career guidance in the late 1950s and 1960s. On the subject of advice, the report distinguishes, as we do above, between advice and counselling though unlike us it chooses guidance as its generic term. We prefer to see guidance used as a more explicit description of the directive position, akin to advice giving rather than as somehow encompassing both advice giving and counselling.

Butler's list bears some resemblance to an earlier classification produced by Watts (1980b). He identified six possible guidance functions:

(a) 'Information' — providing factual detail on options available.
(b) 'Assessment' — evaluating student (client) suitability for options.
(c) 'Advice' — recommending options to meet student needs.
(d) 'Careers education' — defined by Watts as 'providing a programme of planned experiences designed to develop in clients the skills, concepts and information they need to make career choices and transitions.'
(e) 'Counselling' — facilitating the awareness by clients of their own needs and resources.
(f) 'Enabling' — helping clients to implement their choices.

Watts argues that the first three (information, assessment and advice) represent the most widely recognized and widely implemented guidance functions.

CLIENT PROBLEMS AND THE ROLE OF THE PROFESSIONAL

As we indicated in the first chapter of this book, adult life is a period of change or transition or as Adams, Hayes and Hopson define them (see Adams *et al.* 1976) 'discontinuities in people's life spaces'. So when people come to us as educators for information, advice or help we can think of this process as one of transition learning in which, through exploring an area of concern, individuals learn things about themselves which transform them as individuals. Simply to tell a person what to do or just to treat oneself as educator as a parental figure and the client as prospective student as a child figure serves only to reduce the individual seeking help to a position of dependency. It does nothing to foster skills of independence, self-help, decision making, negotiating and coping with anxiety, which will help the person to gain greater self-awareness, understanding and a sense of control over his or her own life and destiny. Seen in this light, an individual's expressed need for educational guidance may be the tip of a much larger iceberg, a symptom of issues that are important for that person at that time in his or her life. Typical adult issues and concerns include:

> anxiety about marriage and preparation for marriage;
> having children and bringing up a family;
> career choice and job change;
> coping with middle age — the so called mid-life crisis;
> preparation for retirement and old age;
> coping with illness and handicap;
> relationships inside and outside marriage.

The list is endless but can essentially be described as concerned with life events and age related developmental stages described in more detail in Chapter 1. It is with contexts such as these that counselling is concerned. Counselling is not some kind of psychotherapeutic panacea for the neurotic or emotionally disturbed. Rather its focus is on normal people experiencing normal problems of living. Watts (1980a) has referred to the idea of guidance functions being directed to adults in the capacity of one of four roles: worker, student, leisurite and pensioner. Perhaps you would like to think about individual adult students whom you have advised in some capacity, or else about your own experiences as an adult student. Against each student list first the educational choices made by that person and secondly the relationship between each choice and the life event/developmental stage in the model noted above. The purpose of this task is to indicate that education does not exist in a vacuum and to reinforce the point that it sets out to meet highly complex emotional needs. Among writers on adult education, Hutchinson and Hutchinson (1978) have expressed this point more explicitly than most.

> There are many possible moments of crisis in adult life, at work, in the home, in social life, that trigger off feelings of inadequacy arising from early educational loss, or today's mounting educational expectations. But they do not call merely for routine information and advice. Deep personal attitudes and feelings are involved, differing from person to person.

The Hutchinsons' work is of particular interest because they lend support to the idea that the counselling function is intimately tied up with the tutor's role and is to be regarded as a basic professional skill of the adult educator. 'It thrives best', they say, 'in the atmosphere of learning.' We very much agree with this assertion. The more that helpers are concerned with teaching skills of decision making or negotiation, the more appropriately can an environment be described as a learning environment. Chapter 4 has developed the point that professional guidance and counselling services should not be seen as representing an opportunity to shuffle off of a tutor's responsibility to think of himself or herself as counsellor. The provision of a formal structure lends support and weight to the expression of a counselling function by the individual tutor, and constitutes a complementary and not an alternative focus for this expression. We support the development of adequately funded formal educational guidance services. We also support the idea that these services should be properly staffed by adequately trained professionals and volunteers. Ideally these persons would possess some sort of idea of learning methodology and the tutorial needs of prospective students. At the same time, we are strongly indicating our commitment to the view that counselling is an important component of the helping skills of all those who would be professionally involved with the education of adults and that a comprehensive counselling provision for adults will involve all these components and not just one or the other.

CONCLUSION

Educational guidance services are needed in order to match resources on the one hand with aspirations on the other. The fact that the latter are often unreal, or unarticulated, or vague, simply highlights the need to see individuals who want help, in a non-mechanical way. This orients us towards considering the matching process as one which involves the wider process of counselling rather than the narrower one of guidance or advice giving. We have articulated this process in detail in Chapters 2 and 3. Suffice it to say here that by allowing and encouraging people to take responsibility for their own decision making, we facilitate their ability to make decisions. This means that skills developed in one problem solving context can be transferred to other contexts. In this sense, therefore, counselling is concerned with helping persons to understand how a solution is reached through becoming aware of the processes which are engaged in, and not just in reaching a solution irrespective of the process. It may help to think in terms of the latter model as an input-output, black box which looks something like this (Fig. 6.1)

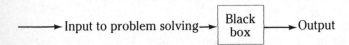

Figure 6.1

The guidance mode, at its most extreme, is not too concerned with the content of the box, provided that a 'result' is obtained in the sense of an output which the students finds satisfactory. In contrast the counselling mode argues that the major gain for the student involves an exploration of the black box, the major component of which is the self of the student. This debate is reflected in the operation of Educational Guidance Services. Some concentrate narrowly on the provision of information, sometimes with a recruitment motivation. Others offer a more objective form of advice or guidance giving. In some, and increasingly this is true of an increasing number of services, a more counselling, student directed approach is being fostered. Increasingly there has also been a growing concern with advocacy, acting on behalf of the student and with systems change as a focusing principle; seeking to amend the system in the interests of the client rather than changing the client so that he or she accepts the system and fits more easily into it.

We have assumed throughout this chapter that guidance services are face to face, but of course as we have already indicated in Chapter 5 contact at a distance is becoming increasingly important. We have already referred to the potential of the telephone system. But a significant new development lies with the growth of interactive computer based systems, particularly if they have the potential for regular updating of their data base. In 1984, Lifeskills Associates (Hopson and Scally 1984), offered what they describe as the first computerized interactive career development programme for organizations. It allows users to develop skills, like objective setting and action planning, at the same time as they are working on a career issue. Hopson points out that 'it includes a customized option to make the program relevant to an individual company's career path and career-development system' (Hopson 1985). Hopson refers to a 'paradigm shift from the Industrial to the Information Era' in describing what is happening at the present time in the area of adult life and career counselling. While the language may be rather complex, there is a lot of evidence which suggests that it is not too far removed from the reality of a rapidly changing situation.

CHAPTER SEVEN

Helping, Guidance and the Question of Work

INTRODUCTION

From early development to late life, work plays an important part in our social experience of the world. The need of labour in order to gain income and begin to satisfy exploratory motives and meet basic needs is a fundamental feature of Western capitalist society. Children play at being workers so as to explore the significance of work (as well as to have fun); adolescents fantasize about work and explore work roles more critically so as to help them in the process of adjustment between school and the world of work or non-work; young adults examine the impact that work has upon them and retired persons speak through anecdotes of their experience of work. Work is a powerful shaper of experience. The average 30-year old with a life expectancy of 74 years will spend 50 per cent of his or her life at work — a total of 174,000 hours. It is not surprising, then, that work shapes experience in such a powerful way.

One of the few British studies to examine the way in which people consider work at different stages of their development was conducted by Hill (1969), who used open-ended interviews with 162 subjects aged between 7 and 20. The findings of this work confirm that perceptions and experience follow a developmental pattern. The children aged 7–9 had both fantasies and observations about work, and these two categories of thoughts were not necessarily linked together. Older children, aged 10–12, showed greater awareness of a wider range of jobs and were aware of differences between jobs in terms of working conditions, salary, training requirements and promotion. Some of these children showed signs of beginning to compare job qualities with their personal attributes. Their descriptions of work and its meaning were still tinged with fantasy. The 13–15 year olds showed more realism and their comments were tinged with anxiety, since work was something they were now having to consider as happening to them — it had more of a personal and emotional meaning for them. This trend — increased personalization of the meaning of work and the layering of this understanding with their own anxiety — is even more marked for the young people aged 16–18. This last group were either beginning to wish that they had spent more time thinking objectively about work or they were trying to make sense of their experience of a job they felt comfortable with but concerned about.

These findings give strong support to a developmental view of occupational choice, which sees thinking about work as being linked to the stage of development the person has reached (see Ginzberg *et al.*, 1951; Super 1957). Such a linking has strong implications for helpers: helping someone look at their career needs to be seen in the context of the stage of development the person seeking help has reached. A further consequence of these observations is that careers related helping is a lifelong process — as the person passes through various life stages they experience changing attitudes and beliefs about work which leads them to re-evaluate their work status. Careers-related helping, if seen from this developmental perspective, is a process that will provide support to a person in need at various times in their life.

In this chapter we shall examine the underlying assumptions about helping that inform careers work and examine the different tasks of the helper at different stages of the persons development. In addition, we shall examine some of the resources available to the person who wishes to engage in this work — tests, computer-assisted services and information banks. Finally, the chapter ends with a brief review of some of the issues which are faced by those people who find their jobs to be unsatisfactory.

An assumption made in this chapter is that many of those who work with adults on career related questions are specialists. These include: career counsellors in local education authorities, personnel officers in industry and business, specialist workers within government schemes (e.g. YTS, TVEI, CPVE) and colleges. Whilst those who are adult educators but not specialists in careers-related work have an important role to play, it is different role from that taken by these specialists. In particular, the explicit role of careers worker carries requirements about the knowledge and expertise that this person should have which are different from those of a subject teacher in an adult centre, leisure programme or extra-mural class. This chapter addresses the specialist role in particular, but makes reference to the role of adult educators and advisors.

Of particular importance to those who are adult educators and non-specialists in careers work is the extent to which their subject provides insights into the world of work. An adult studying a course in engineering benefits from seeing the context in which theoretical and practical knowledge is applied. In doing so, they learn something about careers. Increasingly, as educational institutions are being encouraged and induced to become 'more relevant to the world of work', careers-related education is becoming an implicit feature of many educational programmes. The adult educator's task is to ensure that these implicit features become more explicit: looking at the way in which a particular skill is applied tells us something about the nature of a particular career and both the application of the skill and the learning about career should be explicit features of teaching.

A related function of the adult educator is to motivate the adult learner to question both the nature of work and the meaning work has for a person. Such a task is important for two reasons. First, it encourages the adult learner to see work as something that is not given and has to be taken for granted, but as something that ought to be subject to critical scrutiny. Second, it encourages the adult learner to examine the way in which work affects the way they think, feel and behave. Only by doing so can other changes in the person's life through the life-cycle be understood.

This last point is especially important for women. For many women, work is problematic because of the conflict they experience between work and the pressures associated with childbearing and child care. Our society does not offer financial rewards for the child care work that women do, but instead makes return to work for women who have spent a period away from the labour market more difficult. Adult educators, especially those working on return to learning courses and courses aimed at providing New Opportunities for Women (NOW courses), need to address the way in which gender differences affect the way in which work is experienced.

Finally, adult educators can do much to educate adults on the alternatives to working for others. There is a growing interest in enterprise education, running small businesses and co-operatives. These areas of development — aimed at encouraging entrepreneurship — provide an important teaching area in which the subject matter is the process of working in order to make profits.

THE BASIC ASSUMPTIONS BEHIND CAREERS WORK

In seeking to understand the work that a helper needs to undertake when working with a person concerned about their career development a variety of models have been proposed. All of these models spring from a set of basic propositions which can be summarized as follows:

1 each individual is unique — their personality, emotions and attitudes are shaped by their differing experiences and characteristics;

2 their individual characteristics, coupled with the social circumstances in which they find themselves, qualify each person for a variety of jobs in a variety of work settings;

3 each job has its own characteristic features — different jobs require different attitudes, skills, personalities and physical attributes;

4 vocational preferences and competencies together with a person's social circumstances change during a person's life as they develop and grow through maturity into late adulthood — this implies that vocational choices are made throughout the life cycle, not simply at the end of schooling;

5 the career pattern a person follows (i.e. occupational level attained, the frequency, duration and sequencing of jobs held) is determined by the occupational history of the person's parents (see Willis 1977), mental abilities, personality characteristics, manual and related skills and the extent to which they are exposed to opportunities;

6 the process of vocational development (and, by implication, the task of helping) can be seen as one of implementing the self-concept — the self-concept a person has needs to be linked to their experience of the social world in such a way that their job or work-pattern or career choices reflects as much of 'themselves' as is possible. To some extent,

however, parts of the self will always be frustrated by the
tasks a worker has to complete — there can never be
complete matching — and for this reason, the person needs
to develop a role as a worker;

7 the degree of satisfaction a person attains from their
experience of work is related to the extent to which they are
able to use work as a basis for implementing their self-
concept — the more 'artificial' work feels to them (the more
they find themselves playing a role which is uncomfortable)
the lower is their satisfaction;

8 work and occupation provide the basis for a great many
people (though not all) to structure their social and personal
life and to organize their personalities. This means that some
of the time of the helper is sometimes needed to 'unravel' the
link between work and personality when other social situations emerge as focal points for the personality to express
itself.

These basic propositions need a little more explanation, but they are
presented here in list form so as to provide a 'snapshot' of the ideas
behind this section.

It may seem that one implicit feature of the assumptions listed here
is the idea that career choice is a wholly rational process. It is not. A
great many career decisions are made on the basis of emotions,
chance encounters or decisions made without careful reflection. This
is why emphasis is given in this listing of assumptions to those situa-
tional factors which are seen to be important in shaping career
decisions. It is worth noting, however, that a great deal of the work of
in-house careers specialists is given to helping individuals look at
their less rational experiences of work (see Sworder, 1977).

The implications of this listing for those who work as adult
educators is that the process of helping a person think about work
choices is a process of helping the person understand themselves
better — it is not simply a matter of giving advice on the basis of 'if I
were you'. To do so would be to misunderstand the importance of
work-related questions for personal development. Whilst many who
seek help about work choices and the meaning of work require more
information, this information should always be provided in the belief
that the person is asking questions about the kind of life they wish to
lead.

What is implicit in this list is the assumption that helping a person on work-related matters is much more than simply trying to fit a person into available work slots. The task of helpers in this context is much more concerned with the relationship between the experience of work and the personality and self of the person. This might be termed 'counselling for personal development through the experience of work rather than using work as a basis for shaping the person to conform'.

These assumptions for careers work have led some authorities (most especially those associated with the National Institute for Careers Education and Counselling — NICEC) to regard careers related helping as being concerned with four tasks. These are: (a) opportunity awareness — encouraging the person to look at and think about a variety of work options objectively and to enable them to expand their thinking by looking critically at alternatives; (b) self-awareness — encouraging the person to think about themselves and what they expect work to do for them and to look at what they need from work in order to satisfy their basic needs as a person; (c) decision making — to enable and encourage the person to make decisions about work on the basis of a clear understanding of options and consequences; and (d) transition learning — encouraging and teaching the person to learn from each aspect of their work experience so as to help them develop skills for coping with work and to enable them to see work as a vehicle for learning more about themselves. These ideas are explored fully in Watts, Law and Fawcett (1981), but they are in fact simple constructs. Law and Watts (1977) express them in terms of some basic questions that those in need frequently ask — 'Where am I?' (what opportunities are there around me that I can learn about?), 'Who am I?' (what do I know about myself and what more do I need to know so as to help me understand what work might mean for me?), 'What shall I do?' (how can I accept responsibility for the choices that face me now and will face me later in life — how can I make a decision that I can feel comfortable with?) and 'How will I cope?' (what new situations will I meet and what must I learn in order to cope with them?). To these basic questions, commonly used in careers work, we wish to add another frequently heard amongst those for whom we have acted as helpers: 'Who can help me?' (what opportunities exist for others to support me in the career tasks I have?). This last question is essentially a question about social support and trust. It is a part of the task of the helper to assist the person look at their opportunities for social support both within and beyond the workplace.

There are some additional questions which relate to helping women think about their experience of and relationship to work. Two are especially important: (a) 'How can I reconcile conflicting demands between family and work?' — an especially important issue for women returning to work after a period of absence which sometimes becomes prominent during the course of some educational programme; and (b) 'How can I become confident to return to work after being so long away from work?' — essentially a question about confidence building. Whilst this is not the place to examine in any detail the special political and personal problems of women in relation to work (Kuhn and Wolpe 1978) or education (Smart and Smart 1978), it is important to recognize that women have especial problems in relation to the experience of work, so much so that they have had to secure a certain level of legal protection for work equality and the right to work whilst caring for their families if they wish to do so.

This, then, is the broad framework of work and careers related helping. In a nutshell: careers workers seek to use the experience of work (or thoughts about work) as a means of helping the person learn more about themselves and reach the best possible compromise between how they feel they would really like to be and the social conditions in which they find themselves.

This same framework is helpful in understanding the different roles adult educators can play at different points in the life-cycle. There need be no difference between the nature of the helping process for an adult edcuator and that used by a specialist careers worker. For example, adult educators can do much to promote enhanced opportunity awareness both through the way in which they teach their subject (e.g. by showing the relevance of ideas or skills to work settings), they can help the adult improve their decision making skills by making the decisions about learning that they are required to make more explicit, and they can encourage the development of self-awareness through the way in which they teach and assess learning progress. The helping tasks outlined here are, in many ways, educational tasks — they are the basis of careers education and as such are relevant to all adult educators.

METHODS OF CAREERS HELPING

If you look carefully at the adjectives used in the last section when helping was being described the words 'encourage', 'enable' and 'teach' were used. This reflects the view that careers work is broadly concerned with helping the person reach their own decisions about how they can best 'fit' themselves into the social world of work. Another way of expressing this is to suggest that a great deal of the work undertaken is non-directive counselling insofar as this term implies· that the helper is seeking to actively encourage independence by the person in need rather than seeking to be prescriptive or determinist.

But not all careers work is non-directive. For example, a great deal of work with young people under the aegis of the Youth Training Scheme (YTS) is founded on the social skills model of helping (see Murgatroyd 1985). Individuals are taught to complete job applications in a way that is appropriate given both their experience and the job they are applying for.

Others are given instruction about how to present themselves for interviews — the idea being that there are skills associated with interviewing which, once mastered, increase the chances of the person being able to obtain a job in which they have an interest. Such activities are counselling activities — they seek to enable the person to maximize the opportunities available to them by encouraging them to think carefully about the ways in which they present their 'self' to others. They are based upon the idea that one role the helper needs to play when working with individuals or in groups is that of teacher (or, more grandly, a psychological educator) to ensure that basic skills are learned.

The competent helper in careers work will be in a position to choose between a variety of approaches depending upon the circumstances of the person in need and the contract that they negotiate. Amongst the relevant skills the helper needs are: (a) the ability to give reinforcement to the person once they have made a decision or have expressed a clear view; (b) the ability to teach the person some basic skills, such as those just mentioned; (c) the ability to offer the person an interpretation of their situation; (d) the ability to suggest alternative courses of action for the person; (e) being able to give appropriate and accurate information; (f) being able to use and encourage the person in need to use reflection (of both feeling and content), summaries, clarification and confrontation; and (g) to undertake these tasks within the framework of empathy, warmth, genuineness and concreteness so essential to all helping work. It will be seen that these skills are no different from those needed in other settings described in this book. What is essential, however, is that the helper seeks to make the experience of being helped as concrete as possible.

These activities can be undertaken in a variety of different ways. They can be undertaken on a one to one basis. Alternatively, they can be undertaken through some kind of group work, as is commonly the case in schools, colleges, YTS and in work-study groups within companies. In this latter case, the helper will need some additional skills. These include: (a) a knowledge and understanding of group dynamics — communication, decision making, role and game playing, power and interpersonal processes within a group; (b) an ability to use the group for experiential learning so as to test out skills and ideas in the 'here and now'; (c) the ability to create a climate of social support within a group; and (d) the ability to ensure that individual needs are recognized within the context of the work of the group. Some further skills are given in Murgatroyd (1985) and Hopson (1977).

Not all careers work is undertaken by professionals. Hopson (1977) points out that a large number of individuals meet their needs through peer counselling — counselling by colleagues and work associates. Indeed, a variety of studies show that the peer group is a vital source of information, advice and support for many of those worried by career related matters (Veness 1962). One task a helper has within an organization is to enable individuals to benefit from peer support and counselling.

Not all of the work of the careeer worker that can be seen to be linked to careers and the experience of work concerns work choices or career development. Some of this helping work is concerned with the problems that work gives rise to for the individual — occupational stress, feelings of frustration or failure, feelings of being underused or having overreached oneself are all common problems presented to helpers. In addition, problems that the person experiences outside work which effect their performance at work are also common — marital difficulties or health problems being frequent. Since careers work is just as concerned with the whole person as any other form of helping, helpers who see themselves primarily focusing upon work-related issues needs to anticipate this breadth of presenting problems.

A great deal of the work described here takes place within work settings. Gilbert (1977) documents three pioneering services at Shell UK, Guy's Hospital Group and Heathrow Airport. Other companies have followed these examples and are implementing whole-company counselling services, with ICI, Control-Data and Marks and Spencer UK being at the forefront of this work. Organizational practices vary, but a great deal of effort of these in-house counselling services is given over to adjustment issues (in relation to new recruits or job changes within the company), preparation issues (especially in relation to retirement) and training (especially in relation to human relations skills and communications). In addition, most services take the view that private troubles are sometimes matters requiring policy changes within the company and seek to ensure that the company remains sensitive to the needs of the workforce. Indeed, given that a great deal of contemporary management thinking places emphasis on 'productivity through people' (Peters and Waterman 1982), it is not surprising that an ever growing number of large corporations are investing in counselling and support services for staff.

Having made these general comments about counselling and helping for work-related issues, it is appropriate to observe that a con-siderable effort is made in most parts of Britain to deliver help and guidance services on work-related matters to young people both at school and in the period between school and the establishment of a career pattern. Almost all schools have a designated careers teacher or careers guidance worker, though the quality of the training these staff have received for this work is open to question. Every Local Education Authority has a careers guidance service which has a statutory responsibility to offer careers guidance to young people and adults, though they differ in the way in which they make their services available to adults. In addition, the Manpower Services Commission (MSC) operates a number of schemes for careers advice and training. In addition to the Youth Training Scheme there is also an Enterprise Allowance Scheme aimed at encouraging entre-preneurial activity and a Community Programme, all of which are intended to have a learning and counselling component. The MSC also operate the Professional and Executive Register (PER), which makes available careers assessment and counselling, and the Job Centres.

A number of private consultancy companies exist to give advice and counselling to a variety of individuals on career-related matters. Such companies have developed specialized services both for companies and individuals in relation to 'redundancy' counselling and several operate schemes for assessing an individual's career potential and interests using new technologies and standardized

psychological assessment instruments. Such persons need no qualifications to establish such services, since the terms 'counsellor' or
'psychologist' can be used by anyone (irrespective of their qualifications or training).

Some ethical issues can arise from time to time for a helper who
works for the same employer as the person they are helping. For
example, when a person offers comments about the way they are
treated by a supervisor or manager which reveal that this manager is
behaving in an inappropriate way what action should the helper
take? Alternatively, if the person being helped indicates that they
have a drinking problem or feels unable to complete the job they
have been asked to do, what role does they have within the
company? Such issues, according to Hood, Hollingsworth and
Bannister (1977) do not arise very often. When they do, the counsellor needs to negotiate a clear contract with the person in need
about disclosure and the actions they intend to take so as to ensure
that the long-term well-being of the client is not damaged. A failure to
act in this way can mean that the counsellor becomes a further
problem for the person in need to deal with. Similar issues sometimes
arise for adult educators — especially those engaged in training work
within a company or in day-release or part-release programmes.
Indeed, it is often said that those offering such learning experiences
have more access to the thoughts and feelings of workers than those
in the works personnel departments. The ethical practices of helpers
and educators should be the same: disclosure is a matter for each
helper to determine each time it becomes an issue and should be
undertaken only after the intention to disclose is made known to the
person who is most directly concerned — the person in need.

TECHNICAL RESOURCES FOR HELPING

Careers-related helping, counselling and guidance workers have
developed — more than many others engaged in helping adults — an
array of technical resources to assist them in their tasks. Prominent
amongst these resources are psychometric tests which seek to
measure job satisfaction, the abilities and aptitudes of an individual
and personality: job matching schemes. Given the developments in
computer technology, a great many of these instruments are now
computerized.

In a recent review, Sampson (1984) draw attention to the variety of computer systems for careers guidance which have a more recent history than the even larger number of such systems for careers information. Computer guidance systems enable the person whilst on-line to the computer to engage in activities which help the person clarify their expectations about work (self-awareness activities) whilst at the same time teach the person some decision making skills. In addition, the computer's capacity to search information files and link career opportunities with both the self-knowledge and the decision making the individual has engaged in is a powerful (if initial) way of promoting opportunity awareness. Such a use of technology can render one-to-one helping and counselling a much more concrete activity. Interested readers are referred to the reviews of such services by Harris-Bowlsbey (1984), Heppner (1985), Katz (1984) and Pyle (1984). What they will find on reading these materials is that the most sophisticated services are available in the USA and Canada and that Britain has only a small number of small-scale projects along these lines (Watts and Ballantine 1983).

Having said this, there have been some recent developments in the technical capacity of one system — Job Ideas and Information Generator Computer Assisted Learning (JIIG–CAL) — which are described fully by Closs (1986). At this time, JIIG–CAL is primarily intended for adolescents and school leavers, though an adult development is planned which may be accessed through PRESTEL or home micro-computers equipped with the necessary hardware to run JIIG–CAL. Indeed, there are a number of information and choice packages now developed for use on the BBC Micro produced by the Careers and Occupational Information Centre (COIC). These include Computer Signposts with Job Ideas', and 'Pathfinder', both of which aim to promote self-awareness and decision making. These stand-alone computer services contrast with others that are intended to facilitate counselling by an experienced counsellor. For example, Hopson and Scally (1984) have developed a program known as 'Career Builder' for use by counsellors in work settings which helps the person in need and the professional counsellor identify issues requiring counsellor attention.

Technical support is not restricted to computer based guidance or information systems. A large number of pencil and paper tests are also available. These include the Strong-Campbell Vocational Interest Inventory (Strong and Campbell 1977) in which an attempt is made to link expressed attitudes with specific careers (this is also attempted in a computer scoring system known as CASCAID-HE for adult students which is widely used by the Open University), and the Career Development Inventory (Super, Kidd and Watts, 1977) which seeks to examine the person's thinking about career in relation to their stage of development. There are many more, some designed for special populations (e.g. physically and mentally handicapped people) and others for specific age groups.

Further technical support comes from information banks which produce their materials in print form. Of particular value are occupational guidance information booklets published by the Occupational Information Service. University and polytechnic careers services (including the Open University) have also developed information banks which are invaluable both to the counsellor and those they seek to help.

All of these services are intended to provide support which complements that given by a person (the counsellor) interacting with another (the person in need) when exploring a matter that is of concern to them both.

CAREERS WORK AND THE LIFE CYCLE

Having described the resources and styles of careers- and work-related helping it is now time to examine the practice of such helping in more detail.

One way of doing this is to examine the kind of questions which helpers can explore with those they are helping under the headings we indicated were central to careers-related helping — opportunity awareness, self-awareness, decision making and transition learning. This is attempted by Watts, Law and Fawcett (1981) in the context of school counselling, and Hopson (1985) offers some invaluable questions in relation to transition learning. Rather than adopt this approach, the pattern adopted in Chapter One is followed, so that a life-cycle approach is taken here so as to show how the work of the helper changes with the stage of development a person has reached. In the description provided here, the stages of development used by Donald Super — America's leading career development theorist — are used.

Stage 1: Growth

At this stage (ages 5–14) the person begins to explore the meaning of work through fantasy and play. Such role plays are based on idealized understanding of work (often gained from television and radio) and insight derived from hearing others (especially parents and older brothers or sisters) talking about work. In addition to fantasies about work, young children have certain limited knowledge about work at this age.

One valuable career development task that can be performed by a parent or teacher or helper at this stage is to encourage the fantasy exploration of jobs and work situations beyond routine child games. An example is to encourage the person to play a worker they have not played before (butcher, gardener, doctor, solicitor, lorry-driver, salesperson, watchmaker, etc.) whilst at the same time gently questioning their taken for granted assumptions about the meaning of work and the rewards of work. The career counsellor working with children aged 5 to 14 will also provide more and more information about work as the child becomes adolescent. This can be done directly (by telling) or indirectly, through books and materials which help the person think about the meaning and nature of work and specific occupations.

Stage 2: Exploration

As the adolescent enters the period when discussions about work are also anxiety-provoking (they have to make career decisions at this time), then the helper begins the real careers work. This involves encouraging the person to develop self-awareness through self-examination and looking carefully at the way others seem them. In addition, the individual needs to begin to gather in a systematic way information about possible occupations. They also need to discuss occupational choices with others (parents and advisors of various kinds, including their peers) and to seek out relevant work experiences (via summer work, work experience schemes such as YTS, and casual work). This exploratory period can be short or long, depending upon the person's social circumstances. It does not end with the first job a person takes — one strategy young people some-times adopt when starting work is to make a number of changes in their job until they find what they regard as an acceptable level of job satisfaction (a strategy made difficult at a time of high unemployment). Super suggests that the period between aged 15–24 are the years of exploration.

This description ties well with Erikson's developmental task model for this age (see Chapter 1) which suggests that adolescence is characterized by role experimentation, the development of self-awareness, coming to terms with authority relationships and dealing with issues of identity in general. These features characterize the early period of exploration. When the person begins to feel settled in their work, exploration takes the form of looking at the relationship between work and domestic life and looking at the nature and meaning of ambition. Work becomes important in addressing issues about isolation, involvement and intimacy — a feature of Erikson's view of the young adult period (see Chapter 1).

Stage 3: Establishment

Once the person begins to feel that they have made a decision about their career or work pattern, then they seek to become established and secure in that position (ages 25–40). They may seek to acquire appropriate skills needed for promotion or to improve their feelings of job satisfaction by working on their social and communication skills. In addition, they will wish to explore opportunities for job advancement and development through promotion and job changes.

Much of the helping undertaken at this time is given to offering guidance about available opportunities for education, training and promotion, and to exploring with the person the implications of changes in job and work patterns. It is a time when decision making and transition learning skills are at a premium, and helping activities tend to focus upon these tasks. The helper often finds him or herself pushing those they are helping, to consider more information or to take more account of previous experiences when making decisions; and is thus seeking to exert an influence over the process of decision making rather than the outcome.

Stage 4: Maintenance

Once the person has achieved a number of their work-related ambitions, the opportunities for job change and promotion decline. In the mid-life decade (40–50) the person is maintaining their work and seeking to remain secure. This can be a difficult time for many people, as they can begin to feel frustrated about the opportunities they have missed or feel that they wish to change the balance between work and other aspects of their life. An adjustment they have to make is to stability of life, with the quality of life being very tied to the quality of relationships the person has and the extent to which they feel their skills to be used. Erikson characterizes this period as one of 'generativity vs. stagnation' (see Chapter 1). This is an especially important issue for women who, at this age, are often considering returning to work and find many avenues of career development closed to them. The generativity vs. stagnation theme identified by Erikson is often coupled with new understanding of gender differences in the level of access to educational and social opportunities.

The helper during this phase of development needs to help the person further develop their understanding of self in the context of social conditions and development. They need to help the person recognize those things at work and out of work that give satisfaction and explore ways of increasing the frequency and intensity of these occurrences. They need to help the person address questions about the relationship between work and family, work and leisure, and promote the idea that stability is not necessarily stagnation. In particular, a great many creative talents become released during this period of life (for a discussion, see Sheehy, 1982 esp. pp. 76–102); and the helper needs to help the person relocate the meaning and purpose of work for them.

Stage 5: Re-adjustment

In the latter stages of working life (50–75) the person seeks to adjust to the expectation of retirement and then to the reality of being out of work. This brings with it many problems of adjustment including boredom, feelings of isolation, loss of income and changes in status, a lack of structure to time and a renewed quest for meaning (elaborated in the next chapter). Erikson characterizes this period as one in which there is a tension between maintaining one's integrity as a person and falling into despair (see Chapter 1). It is precisely this issue that occupies a great deal of time in working with those who are about to retire (especially those considering early retirement), or in acting as a counsellor to those who have retired. At the core of the helping task is a concern for the person to re-evaluate self and to maintain a view of themselves as having integrity and purpose whether or not they are in work. This is not an easy task. State pensions (especially for single and divorced women who have not worked for a large portion of their lives) are a poor substitute for a wage, and little political or social status is afforded to old age pensioners (known as 'seniors' in most European countries and the Americas). Indeed, our 'seniors' have so little status and income that it is not surprising that the integrity vs. despair issue figures prominently in work with older persons.

Some companies have developed specific programmes to help staff with retirement questions. These include BP, Marks and Spencers, the Armed Forces and the Civil Service. Such programmes seek to maximize the potential of the work setting for counselling, training and life-skills teaching. An Open University course 'Planning Retirement' is widely used in this context too.

These comments about the role of the helper at different stages in the life cycle give emphasis to the developmental nature of careers work. At all these stages the helper can assist by giving information, helping the person assess their attitudes, skills and knowledge, giving advice, enabling the person to make decisions, and teaching and encouraging self-awareness. Such helping has at its core a concern to help the person see work as a means for the expression of self, wherever this is possible.

WORK PROBLEMS

Not all of the problems which those in need present are of the kinds described here, though these are the 'bread and butter' of specialist helpers. A great many problems arise with the experience of work, most especially job stress.

In recent years there has been a growing understanding that work can be very stressful. McDonald and Doyle (1981), in an excellent study text, outline some of the common causes of work-related stress that may be presented to those who help and teach workers: job insecurity, excessive overtime and irregular shift work, unrealistic deadlines, monotony and routine, working under dangerous conditions (an especial problem for the police and soldiers in Northern Ireland), uncertain responsibilities and poor physical working conditions.

The stress caused by one or more of these factors may show themselves in a variety of ways — headaches, absenteeism, depression, boredom, poor work performance and work rate, alcoholism, excessive smoking, accidents, emotional outbursts, feeling and being isolated. Continued experience of these stressors and these kinds of behaviours can lead to physical ill health and difficulties in the home.

Warshaw (1979) and Howard (1984) offer descriptions of the ways in which the experience of these stressors and strains can be reduced through the systematic teaching of skills and through the re-design of the work place by means of quality circles and 'quality of working life' terms within a company or organization (see also Crocker, Charnley and Chiu 1984). Some of the employee counselling programmes mentioned above also deal with these kinds of difficulties, both through work with individuals and through seeking to improve working conditions. There is not the space here to describe in detail the ways in which such services operate (but many of the skills outlined in Chapter 3 on counselling in action are appropriate for this task). The point to note is that many of the developmental features of help seeking in relation to work are just as likely to be expressed through a concern with work stress as they are in the concern with promotion, retirement or job change.

Cooper and Davidson (1982) highlight the special problems which women managers face when seeking to develop their careers and suggest that women managers have inherently more stressful careers than their male counterparts. In part this is because women in management are still relatively rare in Britain (only 8.5 per cent of British managers in early 1981 were female) and face barriers to their career development in a male-dominated territory. But it is also because of conflicts between their role as family members and workers and the difficulties which some experience in personal relationships at work (sometimes expressed in terms of sexual harrassment). Women in work may need help to explore these issues for themselves, and may need information about the way in which others are tackling these issues within their organization and place of work. Cooper and Davidson (1982) offer some information about the attempts of enlightened work organizations to assist women with these difficulties through the provision of support services and the development of company policies which support women, and more up to date information can be obtained from women's groups and organizations. Most critical, as far as helping is concerned, is that women who present with difficulties of this kind are accepted and given support, and that their confidence in their own thoughts and feelings is encouraged to develop. The helper's task in these circumstances is to help the person in need face up to the reality of their situation and to give them some confidence to begin to take steps to obtain personal support.

CONCLUSION

Careers counselling, helping and guidance work is a complex area in which there are many skills and resources and many different ideas about good practice. *The British Journal of Guidance and Counselling* frequently carries accounts of such issues, and there is a voluminous careers guidance literature. From our point of view, the concern here has been to present an overview of this territory of work with adults. In doing so, our intention was to make clear that counselling about work cannot be divorced from counselling about self or about social conditions. A clear theme of this chapter is that work-related helping and counselling is as much about the development of the person as it is about helping the person come to terms with the experience of work.

One obvious problem is that not all who wish to work in Britain are able to do so. Indeed, there are almost 4 million people who wish to work but who are unable to do so, and a further number who have retired early or before they feel that they have exhausted their wish to work who would like to find some constructive way to use their time. These issues will be explored in the next chapter. The point to note here is that career and work-related helping and counselling cannot simply be concerned with fitting people into the existing work structure. It is also concerned with helping that structure adjust to the needs of the individuals who are finding it a barrier to their development.

CHAPTER EIGHT

Counselling for Unemployment and Retirement

INTRODUCTION

The previous chapter describes the basic framework for counselling in the context of beginning or continuing employment. The essential tasks are: to assist the person in examining the opportunities available; to explore the meaning of these opportunities in the light of their own self-understanding; to facilitate the making of decisions and to explore the issues which will or can arise when the person seeks to adjust and cope with a new work situation. Implicit in these tasks is the idea that counselling, helping and guidance work seeks to explore the meaning of work for the person and the implications of career for personal growth and development throughout the life cycle.

But not all those who seek the services of adult educators, occupational guidance workers, careers counsellors or helpers at work are in employment. Indeed, a great deal of the work of local authority careers services in Britain and adult educators working on Youth Training and other government schemes is concerned with *un*employment. In addition, many of those who act as helpers in the work setting are concerned with preparing staff for unemployment (when enforced or voluntary redundancy takes place) or retirement. A significant agenda for such counsellors and guidance workers is 'coping with non-work'. This is the concern of this chapter. In addition to exploring the impact of non-work on the person, the chapter will examine the strategies which counsellors and helpers can and do use when working with the unemployed. Attention will be given to the value of social and life skills training as well as to educational counselling for those who seek such help.

Before examining the nature of the experience of becoming and being unwaged, there is a need to set in context the work of adult educators and other helpers. Unemployment has social, medical and psychological consequences. The undesirable consequences of becoming unwaged give rise to requests for help which are serious and demanding of professional and volunteer counsellors in a variety of public and private agencies. But unemployment is *not* primarily a psychological or educational issue. It is a political issue. Unemployment arises for a variety of reasons — political decisions made by governments in this and other countries, aggregate demand and supply of products create the demands for labour within capitalism and therefore affect the level of employment in a particular country. Local employment is a function (in part at least) of the decisions taken by local government. Helpers need to bear in mind these points when they work with the unwaged, since many of them assume that they themselves are to 'blame' for being unemployed or unwaged. Helpers need to ensure that the person who feels and thinks this understands the political and economic basis of his or her problem.

Throughout this chapter we will examine the role of a variety of helpers — adult educators working with the unwaged and unemployed, counsellors in centres for unemployed persons, voluntary workers and others. Our assumption is that a great many of those who work in educational institutions, social agencies and voluntary organizations have a helping role in counselling and guiding unemployed persons. Our task in this chapter is to set this work in context and to indicate ways in which this work can best proceed.

BEING WITHOUT WORK

When a person is working there are a number of explicit and implicit features of work that bring personal and social benefits. Work provides income. Such income can help the person meet basic needs for shelter, heat, light and food as well as assist in the pursuit of other activities including education and leisure. Work provides structure and shape to time. Work determines the beginning, middle and end of a day or a working week; it provides a framework to contrast work and leisure or work and holiday; it enables the person to differentiate between time which they control and time which is controlled by the demands of work. Work provides the person with status. When you first meet someone there is usually a question about work ('What do you *do*?') since a person is frequently categorized by work status. Indeed, many people introduce themselves to others as workers of a particular kind, and this suggests the importance of work in shaping social status. Work provides a focus for communication and interest — it occupies so much of a person's waking time and enables them to be active and feel engaged in some task. Finally, work provides a basis for contact with other people.

When a person finds themselves without work, whether because of retirement or unemployment, they experience the antithesis of these features. According to Marsden and Duff (1975), the unwaged experience the following:

Boredom: Because of the loss of focus for their activities and the relative absence of time related and task demands, the person is more likely to be bored;

Isolation: Not being at work means that the person is isolated from colleagues and has a smaller circle of regular contacts (many friends cannot be visited as they are at work). What is more, many of those who are available are also unwaged.

Relative poverty: Being unwaged (if it means reliance on state benefits) means that the person experiences a significant loss of earnings which in itself acts as a further social inhibitor. For example, leisure pursuits are generally expensive in terms of both travelling costs and fees.

Shapelessness: Work is no longer the shaper of time and experience — each day has a similar shape and time is not divided into work and non-work. This renders days, weeks and months shapeless.

Loss of self-esteem: All studies of unemployment which have used psychological methods find that those who have been unemployed for ten weeks or more experience a loss of self-worth and a degree of guilt about their situation. This is compounded by their feeling that work provided them with status and that this status is threatened when work is removed.

Entrapment: Because of relative poverty and their isolation many unemployed persons feel trapped in this situation. News of available jobs spreads first amongst those who are employed — by the time it reaches the unemployed they are often too late to benefit from this word-of-mouth advertising. Their own social contacts tend to be predominantly other unwaged persons who are often unwilling to share information about available work in case this jeopardizes their own chances of returning to employment. This feeling of entrapment, reported by some of the unwaged studies, further lowers the self-esteem of the person.

Much of the writing about the position of women in our society reflects these same six features. For example, Smart and Smart (1978), Zaretsky (1976) and Rice (1981) all provide research studies which exemplify the way in which these feature of being unwaged affect women and make their return to work or the experience of satisfaction with their non-work roles difficult.

Whilst the experience of being and becoming unemployed varies from person to person, it will contain some or more of these elements. These descriptions also apply to many of those who retire, especially those who feel that they are being retired before they themselves feel they are ready to do so.

These social and psychological features of becoming unemployed are seen to be linked to a further set of consequences for the unemployed. It is that becoming unemployed has physical consequences too. Cobb and Kassl (1977) have shown that becoming unemployed can increase the risk of coronary failure, increase the likelihood of a person becoming arthritic or diabetic, and increase their susceptibility to gout, hypertension and peptic ulcers. Work by Jacobson and Lindsay (1979), confirmed by Smart (1979), also shows that the incidence of alcoholism amongst workers who are long-term unemployed is higher than expected, despite their economic circumstances.

Not everyone experiences job loss in these ways. Schlossberg and Leibowitz (1980), when noting the way in which the person's own level of social support can moderate the effects of these negative features, suggest that there is a typology of persons best able to cope with becoming unemployed. These persons are: (a) able to achieve support and affection within their family — they have intimate family relationships which are supportive; (b) sustained by a wide network of social relationships — friends, former work colleagues, relatives; (c) benefiting from institutional support in the form of training in new skills (including social and life skills), and they are being helped with information and advice about their benefit entitlements and the nature of available work; and (d) used to coping with difficult situations and find them to be challenges rather than threats — they have a large coping repertoire. Whilst such people are rare, there are a number of persons who find short periods of unemployment enabling rather than disabling; it permits them to undertake tasks, to reflect or to acquire new skills in a way that is difficult whilst in employment. The work of Schlossberg and Leibowitz (1980) carries many implications for adult educators, not least of which is the need to develop institutional supports for those who are being made unemployed, and the need to complement or help to create social support networks as part of their strategy for helping the unemployed. Indeed, one critical role for adult educators is to offer their physical plant (meeting rooms, transport and other resources) so that people who wish to network and create opportunities for self-help and mutual aid can do so at low cost.

ADJUSTING TO NON-WORK

When a person loses their job, either through redundancy or retirement, there are a number of reactions that take place. These reactions vary in intensity and sequence: different people experience these feelings and thoughts in different ways. Murgatroyd and Shooter (1982) (documented fully in Murgatroyd and Woolfe 1982), suggest that this sequence of experience is essentially a form of grieving. As such they suggest that there is a six-stage developmental sequence of grieving in relation to the loss of a job. These stages are:

1 *Loss*: Whether the job loss has been anticipated or not, the first experience reported is a sense of loss, both in terms of work as an activity and in terms of the security that being in work offered them. As one former personnel manager said 'It is as if I have lost a limb — it has changed what I do, when I do things, how I am and how others see me . . . I feel disabled, just as if I had actually lost a limb!'

2 *Searching*: The feeling of loss (which can involve anger, sadness, guilt, frustration and disbelief) soon merges into the task of searching. Most researchers and observers have focused upon job search activities as indicative of this stage, but other forms of search are also engaged at this time. These include such searches as that 'for the real me' (an identity search), 'for the me I would really like to be' (a fantasy search) and for new means of survival and income generation (a survival-security search). Not all of these are intended to lead to definite outcomes. All are, however, concerned to boost the self-esteem of the person. Only the search for security and survival is pursued with vigour by almost all those who

find themselves without work. What is important to note is that all these searches are intended to lead the person to feel more positive about themselves. What is more, most of the searching activity involves action — it keeps the person active.

3 *Re-Finding*: After a period of searching for meaning and activity, the person enters a phase in which they seem to have found some purposive activity that occupies them for substantial periods of time. For example, they may re-decorate their house or engage in detailed planning for an extended holiday. Alternatively, they may find themselves working in the 'black economy' doing jobs for cash for others without the security of continued employment. Most typically, the re-found 'work' is a poor substitute for the person's previous employment and its positive effects are soon lost.

4 *Re-Loss*: Though the re-found work temporarily acts as a substitute for the 'real thing', it soon becomes clear to the person that the work they are engaged in is not 'real work'. This realization that temporary work, unpaid work for friends and relatives or work in the black economy is insecure and not an adequate substitute for paid employment leads to a difficult period in the person's experience of being unemployed. It is at this stage that many of the most severe effects of unemployment begin to be seen. These include: (a) a denial of the consequences of being unemployed especially as it affects the immediate family of the unemployed person; (b) withdrawal from the task of finding work or of adjusting to retirement, accompanied by depression, lethargy, physical illness or excessive drinking; (c) the development of learned helplessness (Seligman, 1974); (d) the 'freezing of emotions' in an attempt to immunize themselves from further painful reactions to being unemployed; (e) hostility towards others, especially those who are most supportive within the family; and (f) the development of grief and atonement feelings which often show themselves in obsessive behaviours. These six kinds of responses during this phase vary in intensity, but are frequently seen features of the unemployed person who seeks the help of voluntary counselling agencies or friends. This is the phase at which the person feels most vulnerable.

It is likely that the person will 'switch' between the re-finding and re-loss phases with some regularity. This will continue until the person feels secure, either in retirement, as an unemployed person, or by finding work. The re-loss experience can become very intense when the person finds themselves in and out of a number of short-term temporary employments. It is this switching between the finding and loss experiences which so typifies many grief situations (Murray-Parkes 1972).

5 *Awareness*: The grief work just described can last for some time. The person can be helped (through friends, their own efforts, counselling) to come to terms with their situation and to understand what it means for them to be without work. That is, they can develop a thinking-frame or way of coping which better equips them to deal with the situation in which they find themselves. One consequence of this is that the person seeks out new challenges and tasks which are not being used as substitutes for work but which are being pursued for their intrinsic value; they seek to learn more about themselves and their reactions to situations; they make decisions about the way in which they wish to spend their time and what kind of tasks they are going to pursue, and through these steps become more self-aware. The person puts themselves back in touch with the reality of their situation but does so in a way that is less harmful or stressful to them.

6 *Burial*: This final phase of the process of coming to terms with the loss of work involves acceptance. The person, whether long-term unemployed or recently retired, accepts that this is their situation, that their feelings of anger or pain about finding themselves in the situation will not change it, and that their time can be spent constructively and in relationships with others. In the words of one person we have helped, she decided to 'stop being self-pitying or angry and get on with life in a spirit of challenge'.

Not all those who become retired or unemployed will pass through these phases. Most of those who seek counselling and guidance will, however, be at one or other of these stages. One major task for the helper is to discern just where in this developmental sequence the person is at the time they first present themselves as in need of help.

The position of school leavers who are unable to find work deserves a special mention. In their case, what is lost is not the experience of being in work but the expectations of what work would bring for them. For example, work formally marks a status passage between being an adolescent and being a young adult. It provides income which permits the young adult to develop a social life independently of parents. Work makes the young adult a member of the family with additional responsibilities — the family can become dependent upon his or her income. Work marks the young adult out from parents in terms of the occupation chosen — the choice of occupation reflecting the status aspirations of the young person. Most critically, becoming employed represents a status passage for young people. It is the beginning of a new and major phase of their development as persons. When work is denied to the young person all of these features are affected. The young adult is denied access to many activities which those who did find work can now afford; status in relation to parents becomes ill-defined and this often gives rise to tension; the identity search is made more complex by the absence of a clear social position. Whilst there are a number of schemes for young people (e.g. Youth Training Schemes), these are not regarded as 'real work' or (as yet at least) as real training — they perpetuate the feeling of being 'in limbo' awaiting a development in life.

What then becomes an issue for these young people and their parents (in addition to all those mentioned above — boredom, isolation, relative poverty, shapelessness, loss of self-esteem, entrapment) is the extent to which their expectations of work and the meaning of work are *and have always been* a fantasy. Many young people lose their confidence in their own judgements and their social understanding as a result of becoming unemployed (Marsden 1982). Their previously taken for granted assumptions about their status in society, about the meaning that work would have for them both personally and within the family and the assumptions that they reasonably made about the pattern of their development are all suddenly challenged. Being unemployed as a school leaver breaks the social contract which many young people thought they had with society. The result is that earlier fantasies about work (see previous chapter) are replaced with nightmares about halted development (Marsden 1982).

Young people experience these events in a very particular way within the family. Parents can feel that the fact that their son or daughter is unable to obtain work may mean that they have failed as parents in some way or that their child has failed them. In addition, the increasingly long-term nature of unemployment experienced by some young people puts a strain on the relationships within the family: each day of a young person's unemployment means the loss of an ideal which many parents hold for their sons or daughters. Murgatroyd and Shooter (1982) and Murgatroyd and Woolfe (1985) give case material showing the effects that this can have upon the family as a whole.

The task of the helper in these circumstances is made much more difficult by the family dimension that is central to the experience of most young long-term unemployed people. The helper needs to bear in mind that, in dealing with a young adult who is seeking to come to terms with the experience of unemployment, they are also dealing with the problems of adjustment to loss within the family as a whole (Murgatroyd and Woolfe 1985).

THE HELPING TASK

Given these descriptions of the experience of unemployment and loss of work through retirement, what then is the task of the adult educator, voluntary helper or counsellor?

There are differences between the task of those working with the unemployed person who is seeking work and those working with a retired person or an unemployed person not seeking work. Whilst both will need to deal with adjustment problems arising from the absence of work, for those dealing with retirement this is the major focus for their work; for those dealing with the unemployed person who wishes to work the task of adjustment is only a part focus for the work. In this latter case, the helper also needs to address issues about career development and training if they are to assist the person achieve their aims.

Because of these differences in focus, the remainder of this chapter will draw a sharper division between the unemployed person and the retired person. Whilst the basic features of their experience is, as we have seen above, similar, the differences between these two groups from a practical point of view are significant. In particular, the retired person is seeking to come to terms with generally being unable to apply for work even if they wish to and this in itself is a symbolic statement about the stage of life they have reached.

HELPING THE UNEMPLOYED AS AN INDIVIDUAL

There are several key tasks a helper needs to undertake when working with an unemployed person as an individual when this person is finding that unemployment is something that they can no longer tolerate. In this section we examine these tasks. It is assumed that the tasks we describe will be relevant in different ways to different kinds of helpers. For example, those who are adult educators working in a college or work environment are able to perform some or all of these tasks in a different but complementary way to those who work as specialist helpers in a voluntary agency for the unemployed. The point to note is that the tasks we outline are designed to assist the individual deal with their own 'crisis of unemployment'.

Murgatroyd (1985b), following Schwartz (1971), suggests that the helper has seven tasks to complete when working with a person who is finding their experience of unemployment intolerable:

1 Help the individual face up to their situation — help them understand the reality and discourage exaggeration or starry-eyed notions of what can happen;

2 Break up their experiences into discrete categories — make the experience more manageable by sorting it into 'boxes' (e.g. boredom, relative poverty, thoughts about self, feeling trapped, time and shape) so that they can more readily think about precisely what is happening to them;

3 Stop them guessing and wishful thinking about the future — encourage objective thinking about skill development, job search and their own needs;

4 Avoid false reassurances — as a helper it is important not to make promises or offer hope when these promises cannot be kept or the hopes cannot be realized;

5 Discourage projection — though it is not the individual's 'fault' that they are unemployed (their unemployment is a consequence of a variety of decisions made by others which interact with the skills and personality of the individual), the person is not helping themselves by blaming others and waiting for others to act on their behalf. A helper needs to encourage them to accept *some* responsibility for their situa-

tion and *full* responsibility for the way they feel about that situation;

6 Help the person in need to 'help themselves' — a critical role for a helper is to help the person make good use of the available services and supports in the community. In addition, the helper needs to offer direct skill training (teaching), if the person is unable to access social supports, as a way of helping them meet their own needs;

7 Finally, the helper needs to teach and enable the person to cope with the experience of unemployment by offering them specific ways of shaping their time (to overcome boredom, shapelessness), to maximize the use of their scarce financial resources (to reduce the extent to which the person feels themselves to be experiencing poverty), and to connect them to others (to reduce boredom, isolation and feelings of entrapment).

These seven tasks are easily described but more difficult to perform. They all involve *supporting and accepting* the person in their own right — helping is not made conditional on them searching for or being successful in finding a job. They all involve minimizing fantasy and promoting objectivity. Finally, they all involve the person who is helping in offering to develop skills (of being objective, of facing up to reality, of breaking down complex experiences into manageable doses, of taking responsibility for the way that they feel, and of connecting themselves in a productive way to social support). The tasks are a mixture of counselling and teaching roles.

All of these tasks need to be focused in a specific and concrete way on the situation and experience of the particular person being helped. Even though unemployment is a mass phenomenon, it is experienced in unique ways by each person affected. The helper has to adjust their work, language and the emphasis of helping to the needs of the individual they are helping.

In developing a helping relationship of the kind implied here, it is important for the helper not to over-dramatize the situation. Roberts, Duggan and Noble (1982) as well as Marsden (1982) observe that the impact of unemployment is not to cut the person off from their normal activities but rather it is to scale them down to such a level that the nature of the activities change. It is also worth noting, as does Watts (1981), that many unemployed adults (especially young adults) are able to add to their social benefit payments some income or rewards derived from three rapidly growing sectors of the economy — the 'black economy' (work undertaken wholly for cash which is not declared as income), the 'communal economy' (the production of goods and services in exchange for goods and services) and the 'household economy' (work undertaken in the home that would normally be undertaken by another person or which produces economic benefit to the home). These economic sub-systems are described well by Pahl (1980) and Gershuny (1978). They provide one basis for encouraging the person to seek fulfilment and aid personal survival through the systematic use of one or more of these ways of working. Helping an unemployed person cope with being unemployed need not be synonymous with encouraging them to find work in the formal economy of paid work for establishment companies and large organizations.

Most important of all in helping a person face up to their situation is to get them to do something and to seek pride in what they do (Kelvin 1981). In some senses, it does not matter what they do — making models, taking on voluntary or community service, attending adult education classes for leisure or skill enhancement, decorating the home, making wine and beer — as long as what they do helps them to structure time, alleviate boredom and engages them in a task in which they can take pride in their achievement. If the person can record achievements, then the task of helping is much easier.

There are many structures within which the tasks outlined here can be completed. Some of them can be undertaken by family and friends (especially tasks 1, 2, 3 and 6). Others may require more objectivity and can best be undertaken by a trusted adult who may also be an adult educator, voluntary worker or friend (especially tasks 4–7). Some require information and some use of basic teaching skills (tasks 2, 5, 6 and 7) to be maximally effective, though this does not imply that the helper needs training in order to complete them.

In pursuing these tasks there is a need to attend not only to the psychological and social well-being of the person but also to their physical well-being. The Mutual Support Network in Wales (see Murgatroyd and Woolfe 1982) found it necessary in their work with unwaged and unemployed people to offer help on diet planning and food buying (through a food co-operative created by unemployed people to reduce the costs of eating) as a means of encouraging better health amongst those affected by unemployment. In addition, many found that they were becoming unhealthy in other ways — poor sleep patterns, irregular eating, excessive coffee and alcohol intakes, as well as poor diet. It is just as important to help the person come to terms with the physical implications of unemployment as it is to help them deal with the psychological and social consequences. This can be done through voluntary centres and educational institutions making fitness and health a key issue in their programmes for the unwaged and unemployed.

Perhaps the most difficult task of those outlined above concerns task 4 — discouraging projection and encouraging the person in need to accept responsibility for the way that they feel. It is a subtle point that many helpers seem to miss. Whilst the person is not to be held responsible for being unemployed — they are not simply able to 'get on their bikes and find work' — they *do* have responsibility for the way in which they feel. For the person in need attributes meaning and significance to their own situation; others do not prescribe feeling. Only rarely will an individual find being unemployed liberating or exciting — indeed, none of the respondents in the Roberts, Duggan and Noble (1982) study spoke of unemployment in anything but negative terms. Most individuals seek to maintain their dignity and sense of purpose throughout the experience of unemployment, despite the relative poverty that they experience. But the feelings that they have — anger or acceptance, frustration or liberation, purposiveness or pointlessness, hope or despair — are feelings that are shaped by their own thought and actions. Unemployed people can be expected to be frustrated by their level of income, but the range of feelings that they experience about other issues in their lives are many and varied. Because individuals are responsible for the way that they feel they are also able to change and develop their feelings (Dryden 1984; Frankl 1978). The helper's task is to encourage the person in need to own the way that they feel and, if their feelings towards themselves and others are negative, to take responsibility for trying to change the way that they feel. Some of the skills of rational-emotive therapy and language devices described earlier in this book are helpful in this respect.

One key to successful helping with unemployed persons is to help them manage their time. In part, this involves identifying useful and meaningful tasks for them to undertake. But it also involves teaching individuals the value and meaning of time when time is not structured by work. Some helpful suggestions are given in Lakein (1973) and a series of practical exercises that can be used in helping work are given in Davis, Eshelman and McKay (1980). What also helps is for the helper to use a contract for helping in which time is an explicit component. Such contracts can be helpful in shaping the experience of time for the person in need whilst at the same time structuring the helping relationship.

All of these tasks for helping, whether they are undertaken by a voluntary worker or an adult educator, need to be seen as contributing to the individuals coping with and working through their experience of job loss. It should be remembered that the model of loss outlined earlier in this chapter needs to be worked through by the person if the experience of unemployment is to be beneficial to them in the long term. This means that the helper should expect the person in need to be working through the cycle of experiences described in the loss model whilst they are engaged in the helping process. Indeed, it is often the case that those who require most help are those who are in some ways 'stuck' at a particular phase of the experience cycle (Murgatroyd and Shooter 1982; Murgatroyd and Woolfe 1982).

HELPING GROUPS OF UNEMPLOYED PERSONS

All of these comments about helping relate to work with *individuals*. In the context of *groups* of unemployed persons seeking to work together, the helper's tasks are more varied. All of the tasks outlined up to this point still need to be performed. But there are a variety of additional tasks. In this section we shall explore these and describe the roles that educators and voluntary workers and helpers can play.

One critical task for a group of people who are coming to terms with a new experience is to share the meaning of that experience. The educator or helper has to find ways of making this possible without one person dominating the others or the group becoming insular and anxiety provoking. This is not always easy. There are a variety of techniques for groupwork that can be helpful in these circumstances (see Corey and Corey 1977; Douglas 1968; Murgatroyd 1985).

For groups which intend to explore the meaning of unemployment as a basis for helping each other — what might be called a counselling and support group — Murgatroyd (1985a) provides a series of guidelines which can usefully be handed out to group members before a group begins to work together. They are intended to help individuals within the group to understand the group process. They are not instructions, merely observations about how to make the most out of groups. The fourteen points as presented by Murgatroyd to a group of unemployed persons he worked with are as follows:

- realize that the group is a means to an end and not an end in itself: whilst the group may be important to you, don't lose sight of why you joined or what you intend to gain from your participation in the group;
- you will make the most of this group if you trust yourself to make decisions and by trusting others;
- you and only you are responsible for the statements you make — decide for yourself just how much you will say about something and feel free to decide to say nothing;
- you will get most from this group from participating in it and least by sitting there as an observer — if you want to feel good about the group, get involved;
- a great deal of the learning that will happen in this group might make you feel uncomfortable — this is normal, since it is not often that you are encouraged to examine the way you think and feel *with* others in this way, so expect this to happen;
- don't expect miracles from the group — you will find that it takes time for you to start to feel different, but it is worth persisting — remember, everyone else is in the same position as you in this group;
- expect to discover things about yourself that you did not know, especially when others start to share the way they see you and offer to help you, as they will;
- you must decide for yourself what you learn in this group and what you do with that learning — there is no list of objectives, no learning plan and no statement of what you are supposed to be like after having attended this group — all this is up to you and you are given the freedom to learn;
- listen and attend to others as you would wish them to listen and attend to you;
- if you have a persistent feeling (pleasure, frustration, amusement, depression, anger, delight, concern, sorrow) then express it in a way that is appropriate for you;
- think for yourself — your needs and your thought are what matter to you;

- pay attention to the things that others say about you — if there is a consistent message, decide for yourself what you do with that message;
- don't categorize yourself, the way you think or the way you dress — and don't categorize others — you are a complex person and others can only ever partly know you, but do listen and learn; and finally
- don't be afraid to enjoy the experience of this group — it need not be sad or frustrating — it might also be fun.

The group that this list was given to met over 8 weeks for 2 hours each week. All were unemployed men and women aged between 25 and 35 attending an adult centre day class. During the 16 hours of this group a variety of feelings, issues and ideas were explored. As a result, several sub-groups still meet after a year, and once a year about three quarters of the group meet together. According to diaries kept by participants, the group had the following kinds of outcomes: (a) it helped people realize that, though their experiences had unique qualities, the experience of being unemployed was not all that different between people within the group; (b) there are a variety of ways of coping with the experience of being unemployed, many of which just never occur to you on your own; (c) talking and sharing increases the confidence that can be felt; and (d) the stress of being unemployed is moderated by the support that others can give. On the negative side, this group was very difficult to get started — there was simply no experience (apart from the person leading the group) of sharing in a group and there were many awkward silences and false starts. But this is to be expected with such a group.

Although the group just mentioned operated within the framework of an adult education centre, it was not a traditional adult educational group response to unemployment. There was no explicit teaching of skills or ideas and no specific outcomes expected. Other groups for unemployed adults in education are expected to have outcomes. For example, many groups exist to help women return to work (e.g. Wider Opportunities for Women and New Opportunities for Women) which seek to help women become more confident and assertive through the direct teaching of assertiveness and confidence building skills (Lange and Jakubowski 1980). Other groups seek to help women come to terms with the new technology — for example, there are women's technology centres in both Leeds and Cardiff which successfully offer group development programmes and confidence building to women in new technology who have poor educational backgrounds. In both of these cases, the adult educator has two sets of tasks: the first is to achieve the educational objectives of the programme and the second is to ensure that personal learning goes beyond the subject and is truly learning about self. Often this latter objective needs to be a structured part of the process of learning — participants' diaries, evaluation of the programme and their own abilities to learn, the profiling of their own development during a course or the deliberate discussion of self-development in coun- selling sessions during a course are all ways of structuring this learning.

Another example of group learning is the Co-operative Develop- ment Agency (CDA) which seeks to encourage unemployed adults to create a co-operative business venture. One such venture was the development of a snooker supplies manufacturing co-operative. For this CDA initiative to succeed it was necessary for those in the co- operative to develop a sound business plan — they already had the technical skills for the manufacture of the goods. In addition, the co- operative needed to develop skills in collaborative and co-operative working. To help develop a business plan the CDA had its own staff and consultants who act as business advisers. To help develop the skills of co-operation and collaboration, the CDA asked a counsellor who himself was involved in management training to work with the co-operative. Twice a week for two months the counsellor worked with the eight co-operative members on the development of team building skills (Peters and Austin 1985; Woodcock 1979). Of parti- cular importance in this work were these skills: (a) the skills of effective, open and honest communication; (b) the skill of under- standing problems from the point of view of others, not simply one's own; (c) the ability to stick to the point and remain concrete; (d) the ability to confront others about the business in a way that did not make them doubt the fact that they were still accepted as part of that business; (e) the ability to run meetings that were interesting, varied and purposive; and (f) the ability to engage in a process of team- building that would be on-going in the life of the company. The CDA correctly assumed that one of the reasons why co-operatives some- times fail is not because of poor business planning (though this *is* a critical factor), but because of poor group relations within the co- operative. Here was an attempt to use some basic principles from guidance and counselling work and human relations to help a group of unemployed people start their own business.

In each of the three kinds of groups we have briefly described here — the counselling group, the learning group and the co-operative — there are two points to note. The first is that the outcome of what might be called the 'helping and counselling' component is a matter for the individual participants: there are no set limits to the learning objectives, though the helper or adult educator has some in mind when establishing the group. The second point to note is that, whatever the outcomes a group may experience, the process by which those outcomes have been reached is what is most important for the unemployed person to experience. For it is the process of working in a group that helps the person develop appropriate skills for coping with unemployment (Murgatroyd 1982).

This has not been the place to describe group work skills in detail. Valuable descriptions are given in Douglas (1968), Gazda (1978), Jaques (1984) and Murgatroyd (1985a). Our purpose here is more limited: to indicate ways in which the principles of guidance, counselling and helping apply to a variety of groups for the unemployed. For those groups where counselling is not the primary reason for the groups coming together (e.g. in the case of an adult learning group or a co-operative in development or a group in a voluntary organization), the point is that learning about something (a subject, a skill, running a business) involves learning about 'self' and that this latter kind of learning needs to be regarded as an important vehicle for unemployed persons to come to terms with their experience.

HELPING THE RETIRED PERSON IN A GROUP

Some of the points just made about groups for unemployed adults also apply to helping those who are seeking to adjust to the idea or fact of retirement. In this section we shall examine the roles which adult educators, helpers and counsellors can play in helping a person to adjust and cope with their passage from work to retirement — what has been called the 'institutionalized separation of the individual from his occupational position' (Atchley 1976) — through the use of groups. A later section will examine the role helpers and educators can play with individuals. Throughout, the term 'seniors' is used to refer to retired persons — a practice common in many European countries and in the USA.

A large number of companies (most notably British Petroleum, ICI, and Marks and Spencers) have developed programmes for retirement preparation. Often these are offered in association with local education institutions and/or the pre-retirement association. These programmes are of two kinds: (a) *limited programmes* — where factual information (e.g. about pension plans, social security payment and retirement dates, etc.) is presented through a series of short seminars; (b) *comprehensive programmes* — which go beyond facts and information and seek to encourage the person to think through the implications of retirement for the way they will feel, live and stay well. Both kinds of groups can be found in industry, commerce and the corporate business world as well as in some public agencies. In addition, many adult centres offer courses on planning retirement, and there is also an Open University course of this name.

One of the tasks which the person who is retiring has, as Golan (1981) rightly reminds us, is to come to terms with the past. It involves detaching oneself both from the work role and from the physical and secure attachments that work provides. It involves accepting that, despite all the work that one has undertaken, one is not indispensable, and that what has hitherto been a significant part of life will no longer be there as a regular feature. Group meetings within a company to discuss these aspects of retirement provide the person in the group with an opportunity to discover: (a) that their feelings and thoughts about retirement are shared by others; (b) that there is a potential network of support amongst fellow workers after retirement has taken place if they make an effort to secure that support; (c) that there are some issues on which they would benefit from a more formal educational input — especially in relation to social benefits, health, educational and leisure opportunities; and (d) that the retirement of one family member has an impact on other members of that family. These kinds of learning outcomes are reported from comprehensive learning groups for pre-retirement workers. It is noticeable that almost all of these outcomes relate to the psycho-social aspects of retirement. Indeed, most pre-retirement groups focus upon these themes as an explicit part of their work.

There are clear learning needs amongst the pre-retirement or recently retired adult group that can best be met through group work of some sort. These include: (a) the need to develop lifestyles based on lowered income; (b) the need to be aware of the available opportunities for leisure and education for seniors; (c) the need to fully understand their entitlement to benefit; (d) the need for personal health care in retirement; and (e) the need to come to terms with the ageing process and its physical effects. In pursuing these educational territories of work, adult educators need to be sensitive to the fact that they are working with people with a considerable emotional investment in this learning. Here the subject is their own 'self'. Groups seeking to cover some or all of these topics (and others which the group identifies for themselves) need to allow time for group members to reflect on the meaning of the information, knowledge and skills they are acquiring. That is to say, adult educators need to give their learners time *within the group* to come to terms with the personal implications of their learning. A failure to do so will mean that the full learning potential of such a group will be significantly reduced. Whilst this may be difficult (especially if the group is running in company time and on a limited budget), it is important to recognize the significance and personal meaning of these 'classes' for participants.

HELPING THE RETIRED PERSON AS AN INDIVIDUAL

When a person retires they can engage in a number of different kinds of activities. These can be classified (following Kleemeier 1975) as follows: (a) *work substitute activities* — unpaid activities similar to work, such as volunteering; (b) *leisure activities* — engaged in purely for personal pleasure; and (c) *withdrawal* — doing nothing and expecting nothing to happen. The balance between these three kinds of activities will reflect the individual's response to the experience of job loss.

For many, leisure activities are gradually developed and become a source of structure and activity which alleviates boredom and encourages pride in the completion of a task. Atchley (1976) draws a distinction between leisure activities which are pursued solely for pleasure and recreational activities which are pursued for a specific purpose. Individuals often need help and support in locating the resources for leisure and recreational activities which they wish to pursue. It is an important part of the work of educational guidance services for adults (see Chapter 5) to support the retired person who makes these requests.

In retirement, individuals meet practical problems for which they need help. These include financial problems, problems in ensuring adequate health care and problems in securing domestic services. There are a great many agencies for helping individuals with these kinds of problems — benefit shops, Neighbourhood Law Centres, Age Concern, Citizens Advice Bureaux, pensioner unions and clubs and trade union branches amongst them. The helper in these agencies needs to ensure that the individual they are helping fully understands the advice which they are given. Some agencies always write down their advice to seniors, to ensure that they have time to reflect on the precise advice given. Those who run adult education programmes in which seniors are involved will also be approached for information and advice concerning these issues, and should ensure that they refer the individual to the appropriate advice agency and should check later that they have received appropriate advice that they fully understand.

There are two features of advice giving which seniors often indicate frustrate them. These are: (a) the feeling that they are being treated in a patronizing way by a helper; and (b) the feeling that the information they ask for should be more readily available. The first of these problems concerns the quality of the helping relationship between the advice giver and the person in need — being patronizing is not likely to ensure that the person fully understands or hears the advice or information given. Helpers need to attend to the emotional tone of what is said as well as to the information they are imparting. The second issue here concerns the balance between providing generalized written information and personalized service. This is a difficult practical issue. Whilst much of the advice and information which people seek can be generalized for the purpose of a leaflet or fact sheet, most enquirers require this information to be personalized and made relevant to the particular situation in which they find themselves. Each organization involved in helping the retired person and seniors needs to decide for themselves what the balance between generalized and personalized services should be. In making this decision, the matter of costs cannot be ignored.

These points relate to the seeking of information and practical advice. But these are not the only reasons that seniors seek support and help. A number of support agencies within the community (notably Age Concern and Care for the Elderly) find themselves providing more specialized counselling services. Two issues emerge as particularly important areas of work. These are: (a) concern with physical well-being and the fear of death; and (b) coping with the death of a spouse. Both of these issues are also frequently reported as topics of helping conversations between adult educators and the seniors in their classes.

Both of these issues are sensitive. The helper not experienced in dealing with the impact of death and dying on a person might well find themselves unable to cope with both the nature of the problem presented to them and the demands the person in need makes upon them. There are agencies in the community that can and will help with this problem. One of the agencies is the corps of clinical psychologists skilled in working with the elderly and in dealing with death and dying issues (Shooter 1986). Their services are available through the general practitioner system. In addition, there are two voluntary agencies that have much to offer — the Samaritans and CRUSE — both of which have considerable experience in helping individuals cope with grief.

The fear of dying and concerns about well-being are also common after retirement. In Erikson's model of adult development (see Chapter 1) this latter phase of life is focused upon questions about personal integrity versus despair. When these kinds of issues are presented to a helper then more generalized forms of counselling and helping as described earlier in this book are appropriate. What the helper needs to bear in mind is the difference between common 'folklore' about the ageing process and its effects on memory, mobility, relationships and the ability to learn, and the reality of the ageing process (also discussed in Chapter 1). Many of the suggestions made earlier in this chapter about the counselling tasks for the helper working with unemployed individuals apply here too. What is most critical is that counselling and helping work with the elderly is characterized by respect for them as persons in their own right *as they are now* and not simply in terms of their past.

CONCLUSION

This has been a substantial chapter. It has looked at the way individuals who are without work for different kinds of reason can be helped through educational, guidance and counselling services. Throughout the concern has been to set the tasks of these workers in the context of the experience of being without work — something relatively few of these workers have experienced. In outlining these tasks it is clear that working with the unwaged can be a demanding and sometimes unrewarding task. Caring for and working with the unwaged is not intended as a substitute for an increase in the number of people in work or in the size of social benefits for seniors. There are times when the helper or educator will recognize the limitations of their work. This should not frustrate them; rather, it should help them better identify what it is that they are able to do and encourage them to do this with commitment and skill.

Endpiece

It has been argued in this book that any person who could conceive of himself or herself as a teacher or helper of adults would do well to consider themselves as involved in carrying out a counselling role. We consider, therefore, that such persons could benefit in many ways from an examination of the nature of the counselling process, and in Chapter 2 we have provided a framework for doing this. We have suggested there that counselling is not some kind of arcane pursuit, but on the contrary is something that good educators do almost instinctively. Moreover, to develop basic counselling skills need not be difficult and will certainly help them become better helpers. The fact that for many, even most adults, learning difficulties stem from emotional barriers rather than intellectual deficiencies lends force to this argument.

Inevitably, such an approach has many implications for training helpers of adults and we would like to outline some suggestions for items in a training programme and the philosophy underlying them. Such agenda items would include:

(a) Understanding adult life as a process of development and change and the implications of this for the provision of formal curricula and the enhancement generally of a wide range of learning opportunities for adults outside formal institutions.

(b) Understanding the motivation behind and the nature of adult learning, particularly its emotional base.

(c) Understanding the influences of social, cultural and economic factors upon the willingness of adults to learn and the direction of this learning.

(d) An awareness of the need to develop bridges between the worlds of education and work and personal private lives.

(e) A knowledge of how to work within systems so as to promote organizational change.

(f) An understanding of the complexity of interpersonal relationships and of the important part which qualities such as empathy, warmth and genuineness play in such relationships.

(g) Some expertise in basic counselling skills such as active, attending listening, asking open–ended questions and encouraging specificity and concreteness.

(h) A recognition of the open–ended nature of the helping process and the need for the helper to carry on learning in order to practise it more competently.

(i) A recognition of the role of the self in relationships and an acceptance of responsibility for personal development by the person seeking help.

The philosophy underlying this agenda is that the skilled helper is a person who engages consciously in the process of understanding the learning process. So far as training is concerned, this places an emphasis on experiential learning, utilizing experience as a basic for learning. It is not possible to facilitate an awareness of process in the helper by just giving lectures on how to be a facilitator. What is involved is helping trainee helpers to move back and forward between their own experience and theory in an iterative fashion.

We have defined experiential learning in some detail in other publications (see Murgatroyd 1982 and Woolfe 1986), but would point particularly here to its concern with the *experience* of individuals such as trainee helpers, not just with their participation. Experience is seen as a basis for self-understanding and assessment of an individual's own needs, resources and objectives. Moreover, the individual trainee helper learner is regarded as an active participant in the construction of a learning agenda. What this means is that the power in the relationship between educator and trainee helper, which we can describe as the 'locus of control', shifts from the former towards the latter. In this way the trainee helper can be said to be given more responsibility for the content and rate of progress of his or her own learning. The individual is encouraged to make connections between present, past and future. Learning itself is seen as having a transfer value, by which we mean two things. First, it is possible to transfer to different situations an understanding of the processes of learning, whatever the content. Secondly, this understanding of the process of learning can be passed on in the field, by helpers, to those who come seeking help.

We do not wish to imply that this kind of philosophy and approach to training is one which we have suddenly discovered and of which others are not aware. Indeed this is far from the truth. For example the Advisory Council for Adult and Continuing Education points out that 'any consideration of the staffing and training needed for the development of continuing education raises questions as much about quality as quantity' (ACACE 1982). Reference should also be made to the work of Elsdon (1975) and the Further Education Curriculum Review and Development Unit (Miller 1982). That there is a major need for staff development across the existing range of further and adult education has been highlighted in a series of reports from the Advisory Committee on the Supply and Training of Teachers (ACSTT 1975 and 1978). They focus attention on the need for a more systematic and integrated range of training provision. This has been a major preoccupation of the Scottish Education Department in implementing its 16+ Action Plan (Scottish Education Department 1983). The need is unlikely to diminish. The post-compulsory sector of education is full of new ideas and schemes deriving from the growth in importance of the Manpower Services Commission as a source of funding, the development of new training schemes concerned with management skills and technological updating, and the provision of an expanded range of training opportunities to school leavers. Our suggestions far from representing some esoteric or arcane set of interests, can be seen as a necessary focus for future growth in the area of adult and continuing education.

CONCLUSION

The kind of ideas advocated in this book are not designed to make life comfortable either for the helper or the person seeking help and are not likely to do so. Working in a situation where expectations are more open will present a challenge to both parties. The move away from the helper as expert will create uncertainties, both for helpers and those seeking help. The emphasis will be on the helper moving away from a prima donna position into a more brokering type of role. This will involve being prepared to put the person seeking help in touch with other persons with the same needs as well as with other institutions who seem able to respond to those needs. It will also mean working within institutions so as to create the kind of structures which are responsive to adult needs. From the point of view of the person seeking help, it will mean a shift into a less passive, more active role. He or she is no longer seen as the recipient of help, but as an individual who will be expected to do some hard work in defining his or her own needs, resources and objectives.

In the preface to this book, we explained our selection of the terms helper and 'person seeking or needing help', in preference to the more traditional 'tutor' and 'student' or 'counsellor' and 'client'. We have not always found it easy to stick with these terms and indeed have not always done so. The settings in which adult and continuing education take place are many and varied and it is difficult to find a single uniform terminology that will suit all contexts. Using terms like 'helper' and 'person being helped' is only a means to an end. The objective is to draw attention to basic similarities across a wide range of settings in the relationship between learner and teacher. In all these settings, the goal is:

(a) helping people to help themselves;
(b) helping people to be whole people, to express their feelings and their behaviour as well as their thinking side;
(c) to indicate that the four stages outlined in Chapter 2 and 3 are readily available to those who work with adults as are the skills noted in Chapter 3;
(d) to acknowledge that the process of development and change outlined in Chapter 1 is so often of underlying importance in motivating the behaviour of adults.

The point about this conception of the relationship between helper and person seeking or being helped is that it differs radically from a great deal of conventional practice in the field of adult and continuing education. It treats the learner as an active agent in the learning process, as someone working hard to assimilate new ideas and experiences into an existing pattern of looking at the world. The bringing together of old and new is seen as involving individuals in excitement and risk. It follows, therefore, that the learning process may involve a great deal of anxiety and concern. In this kind of situation, the helper is perceived as a facilitator or enabler. This involves not telling or advising people what to do or how to solve their problems, but rather helping them to develop their own resources in a way that will encourage problem solving. This will involve helping them to explore their feelings so as to increase awareness about emotional needs, thus leading to greater clarity and focus about the choices and options open to them. In this way the individual is helped to make his or her own decisions and importantly not just to make a decision, but to be aware of the emotional and intellectual processes that have gone on in the meantime. In other words, decision making is seen as a process, often consisting of a series of stages. In this way the individual has more chance of transferring the lessons learned in one situation into others — what we describe as transfer learning. The principles of guidance and counselling are essential to this model. They provide the philosophical and practical base upon which a relationship between helper and person being helped can be forged. We have tried in this book to articulate the nature of this relationship, not we hope in just a mechanical fashion, but in a way which offers some kind of flavour of what it feels like to regard oneself as a counsellor.

References

INTRODUCTION

Tough, A. (1976) 'Self-planned Learning and Major Personal Change', in Tight, M. (ed.) (1983) *Education for Adults: Adult Learning and Education*, London, Croom Helm.

CHAPTER 1: ADULTHOOD

Allman, P. (1983) 'The Nature and Process of Adult Development', in Tight, M. (ed.) *Education for Adults: Adult Learning and Education*, London, Croom Helm.

Beard, B. B. (1967) 'Social and Psychological Correlates of Residual Memory in Centenarians', *The Gerontologist*, June.

Berger, P. L. (1969) '*The Social Reality of Religion*, London, Faber.

Cross, P. K. (1981) *Adults as Learners: Increasing Participation and Facilitating Learning*, San Francisco, Jossey-Bass Publishers.

Erikson, E. H. (1950) *Childhood and Society*, New York, Norton.

Freire, P. (1972) *Pedagogy of the Oppressed*, Harmondsworth, Penguin.

Giles, K. and Woolfe, R. (1981) *Personal Change in Adults*, Unit 21 of Open University Course 'Contemporary Issues in Education' (E200), Milton Keynes, Open University Press.

Havighurst, R. (1953) *Human Development and Education*, New York, Longmans Green.

Horn J. L. (1970) 'Organization of Data on Life Span Development of Human Abilities', in Goulet, L. R. and Baltes, P. B. (eds) *Life-Span Development Psychology: Research and Theory*, New York, Academic Press.

Huberman, M. (1974) 'Looking at Adult Education from the Perspective of the Adult Life-Cycle', *International Review of Education*, 20, 2 pp. 117–37.

Hughes, E. C. (1937) 'Institutional Office and the Person', *American Journal of Sociology*, 43, November, pp. 409–10.

Karasawa A., Kawashima, K. and Kashahara, A. (1979) 'Mental Ageing and its Medico-psycho-social Background in the Very Old Japanese', *Journal of Gerontology*.

Leaf, A. (1973) 'Getting Old', *Scientific American*, 229, 3, p. 52.

Leonard, P. (1984) *Personality and Ideology: Towards a Materialist Understanding of the Individual*, London, Macmillan Press.

Loevinger J. (1976) *Ego Development: Conceptions and Theories*, San Francisco, Jossey-Bass.

Mezirow, J. (1979) 'Perspective Transformation', *Studies in Adult Education*, 49, 2, pp. 153–64.

Murgatroyd, S. J. and Woolfe, R. (1982) *Coping With Crisis: Understanding and Helping People in Need*, London, Harper and Row.

Murgatroyd, S. J. and Woolfe, R. (1985) *Helping Families in Distress: An Introduction To Family Focused Helping*, London, Harper and Row.

Neugarten B. L. (1977) 'Adult Personality: Towards a Psychology of the Life Cycle', in Allman, L. R. and Jaffe, D. T. (eds) *Readings in Adult Psychology: Contemporary Perspectives*, New York, Harper and Row.

Open University (1979) *An Ageing Population* (P252), Milton Keynes, Open University Press.

Parkes, C. M. (1972) *Bereavement: Studies of Grief in Adult Life*, London, Tavistock.

Puner, M. (1974) *To The Good Long Life: What We Know About Growing Old*, New York, Universe Books.

Woolfe, R. (1983) 'Counselling in a World of Crisis: Towards a Sociology of Counselling', *International Journal for the Advancement of Counselling*, 6, pp. 167–76.

Wordsworth, W. (1798) 'Lines Composed a Few Miles above Tintern Abbey, on Revisiting the Banks of the Wye During a Tour, July 13'.

CHAPTER 2: WHAT IS COUNSELLING?

Arbuckle, D. (1967) *Counselling and Psychotherapy*, New York, McGraw-Hill.

Bok, S. (1982) *Secrets: Concealment and Revelation*, Oxford University Press.

Brammer, L. M. (1979) *The Helping Relationship*, New York, Prentice-Hall.

Brown, D. and Pedder, J. (1979), *Introduction to Psychotherapy*, London, Tavistock.

Carkhuff, R. R. (1969) *Helping and Human Relations: Volume 1, Selection and Training*, New York, Holt, Rinehart and Winston.

Carkhuff, R. R. and Berenson, B. G. (1977) *Beyond Counselling and Therapy*, 2nd edition, New York, Holt, Rinehart and Winston.

Coping with Crisis Research Group (1986) *Running Workshops: A Guide for Trainers in the Helping Professions*, London, Croom Helm.

Dryden, W. (ed.) (1984) *Individual Therapy in Britain*, London, Harper and Row.

Egan, G. (1975) *The Skilled Helper: A Model for Systematic Helping and Interpersonal Relating*, Monterey, California, Brooks/Cole.

Goffman, E. (1969) *The Presentation of Self in Everyday Life*, London, Allen Lane.

Heron, J. (1977) *Dimensions of Facilitator Style*, Surrey, Human Potential Research Project, in association with the British Postgraduate Medical Federation.

Heron, J. (1978) 'Co-counselling', in Proctor, B., *Counselling Shop*, London, Burnett Books.

Hopson, B. (1982) 'Counselling and Helping', in Hall, J. (ed.), *Psychology for Nurses and Health Visitors*, London, British Psychological Society and Macmillan Press.

Inskipp, F. and Johns, H. (1984), 'Developmental Eclecticism: Egan's Skills Model of Helping', in Dryden, W. (ed.), *Individual Therapy in Britain*, London, Harper and Row.

Jaques, D. (1984), *Learning in Groups*, London, Croom Helm.

Luft, J. and Ingham, H. (1955) *The Johari Window: A Graphic Model for Interpersonal Relations*, University of California at Los Angeles, Extension Office, Western Training Laboratory in Group Development.

Munro, E. A., Manthei, R. J., Small, J. J. (1983) *Counselling: A Skills Approach*, Auckland, New Zealand, Methuen.

Murgatroyd, S. (1982) *Some Definitions of Counselling*, Cardiff, Open University in Wales, mimeo.

Murgatroyd, S. (1985) *Counselling and Helping*, London, British Psychological Society and Methuen.

Murgatroyd, S. and Woolfe, R. (1982) *Coping with Crisis*, London, Harper and Row.

Nelson-Jones, R. (1982) *The Theory and Practice of Counselling Psychology*, London, Holt, Rinehart and Winston.

Nelson-Jones, R. (1983) *Practical Counselling Skills*, London, Holt, Rinehart and Winston

Nelson-Jones, R. (1984) *Personal Responsibility Counselling and Therapy: An Integrative Approach*, London, Harper and Row.

Open University Course P.553 (1984) *A Systematic Approach to Nursing Care: An Introduction*, Milton Keynes, Open University Press.

Proctor, B. (1978) *Counselling Shop*, London, Burnett Books.

Rogers, C. (1957) 'The necessary and sufficient conditions of therapeutic personality change, *Journal of Counselling Psychology*, vol. 21, pp. 95–104.

Rogers, C. (1961), *On Becoming a Person*, London, Constable.

Rogers, C. (1970), *Encounter Groups*, Harmondsworth, Penguin Books.

Smail, D. (1980), 'Learning in Psychotherapy', in Salmon, P. (ed.), *Coming to Know*, London, Routledge and Kegan Paul.

CHAPTER 3: COUNSELLING IN ACTION

Berne, E. (1964) *Games People Play*, New York, Grove Press.

Berne, E. (1972) *What Do You Say after You Have Said Hello?*, New York, Grove Press.

Brammer, L. M. and Shostrom, E. L. (1968) *Therapeutic Psychology — Fundamentals of Actualization Counselling and Psychotherapy*, Englewood Cliffs, NJ, Prentice-Hall.

Corey, G. (1982) *I Never Knew I Had a Choice*, Monteray, California, Brooks-Cole.

Dryden, W. (1984) *Rational Emotive Therapy — Fundamentals and Innovations*, London, Croom Helm.

Egan, G. (1982) *The Skilled Helper*. Monteray, California, Brooks-Cole.

Eisenberg, S. and Delaney, D. J. (1977) *The Counselling Process*, Chicago, Rand McNally.

Ellis, A. (1962) *Reason and Emotion in Psychotherapy*, New Jersey, Lyle Stuart.

Falloon, I., Lindley, P. and McDonald, R. (1974) *Social Training — A Framework*, London, Maudsley Hospital (mimeo).

Frankl, V. E. (1969) *The Will to Meaning*, New York, Signet Books.

Goldstein, A. P. (1975) 'Relationship Enhancement Methods', in Kanfer, F. H. and Goldstein, A. P. (eds) *Helping People Change*, New York, Pergamon Press.

James, M. and Savary, L. (1977) *A New Self: Self-Therapy with Transactional Analysis*, Reading, Mass., Addison-Wesley.

Janis, I. (1982) 'Helping Relationships', in Janis, I. (ed.) *Counselling on Personal Decisions*, New Haven, Yale University Press.

Janis, I. L. and Mann, L. (1982) 'A Theoretical Framework for Decision Counselling', in Janis, I. L. (ed.) *Counselling on Personal Decisions*, New Haven, Yale University Press.

Lange, A. J. and Jakubowski, P. (1978) *Responsible Assertive Behaviour — A Cognitive/Behavioral Procedure for Trainers*, Champaign, Illinois, Research Press.

Liberman, R. (1975) *Personal Effectiveness*, Champaign, Illinois, Research Press.

Miller, J. (1982) *Tutoring — The Guidance and Counselling Role of the Tutor in Vocational Preparation*, London, Further Education Curriculum Development Unit/HMSO.

Munro, E. A., Manthei, R. J. and Small, J. J. (1983) *Counselling — A Skills Approach*, New Zealand, Methuen.

Murgatroyd, S. (1985) *Counselling and Helping*, London, British Psychological Society/Methuen.

Nelson-Jones, R. (1983) *Practical Counselling Skills*, London, Holt-Saunders.

Pinney, R. (1981) *Creative Listening*, London, A to Z Publishing.

Rogers, C. R. (1961) *On Becoming a Person*, Boston, Houghton-Mifflin.

Rogers, C. R. and Dymond, R. F. (eds.) (1954) *Psychotherapy and Personality Change*, Chicago, University of Chicago Press.

Trower, P., Bryant, B. and Argyle, M. (1978) *Social Skills and Mental Health*, London, Methuen.

Wilding, P. (1982) *Professional Power and Social Welfare*, London, Routledge and Kegan Paul.

CHAPTER 4: CONTINUING EDUCATION: LEARNING AND TEACHING IN GROUPS

Abercrombie, M.L.J. (1979) *Aims and Techniques of Group Teaching*, 4th edition, University of Surrey, Society for Research into Higher Education.

Abercrombie, M.L.J. and Terry, P.M. (1978) *Talking to Learn*, University of Surrey, Society for Research into Higher Education.

Beard, R. (1976) *Teaching and Learning in Higher Education*, 3rd edition, Harmondsworth, Penguin.

Beaty, L. (1978) *The Student Study Contract*, University of Lancaster, paper presented at the Fourth International Conference on Higher Education.

Berne, E. (1964) *Games People Play*, London, Andre Deutsch.

Bloom, B.S. (1956) *Taxonomy of Educational Objectives; Handbook 1: The cognitive domain*, London, Longmans Green.

Bramley, W. (1979) *Group Tutoring: Concepts and Case Studies*, London, Kogan Page.

Carkhuff, R.R. (1969) *Helping and Human Relations*, vol. 1: *Selection and Training*; vol. 2: *Practice and Research*, New York, Holt, Rinehart and Winston.

Egan, G. and Cowan, M.A. (1979) *People in Systems: A Model for Development in the Human-Service Professions and Education*, Monterey, California, Brooks/Cole.

Entwistle, N.J. (1981) *Styles of Learning and Teaching*, Chichester, Wiley.

Entwistle, N.J. and Robinson, M. (1976) 'Personality, Cognitive Style and Students' Learning Strategies', in Page, C.F. and Gibson, J. (eds) *Research into Higher Education, 1973*, London, Society for Research into Higher Education.

Entwistle, N.J., Hanley, M., Ratcliffe, G. (1979) 'Approaches to Learning and Levels of Understanding', *British Journal of Educational Psychology*, vol. 5, pp. 99–114.

Fontana, D. (1982) 'Learning and Teaching', in Hall, J. (ed.) *Psychology for Nurses and Health Visitors*, London, British Psychological Society and the Macmillan Press.

Gibbs, G. (1981) *Teaching Students to Learn: A Student-Centred Approach*, Milton Keynes, Open University Press.

Gibbs, G., Morgan, A., and Taylor, E. (1982) 'Why Students Don't Learn', *Teaching at a Distance Institutional Research Review*, no. 1, Spring 1982.

Gibbs, G., Morgan, A. and Taylor, E. (1984) 'The World of the Learner', in Marton, F., Hounsell, D., Entwistle, N. (eds) *The Experience of Learning*, Edinburgh, Scottish Academic Press.

Giles, K. and Woolfe, R. (1981) 'Personal Change in Adult Life', in *Contemporary Issues in Education*, Course E200, Block 4, Unit 21, Milton Keynes, Open University Press.

Holmberg, B. (1984) *Adult Education: Students' Independence and Autonomy as Foundations and as Educational Outcomes*, Hagen, FernUniversität.

Hounsell, D. (1984) 'Understanding Teaching and Teaching for Understanding', in Marton F., Hounsell, D., Entwistle, N. (eds) *The Experience of Learning*, Edinburgh, Scottish Academic Press.

Howe, M. J. A. (1976) 'Good Learners and Poor Learners', *Bulletin of the British Psychological Society*, vol. 29, pp. 16–19.

Inskipp, F. and Johns, H. (1984) 'Developmental Eclecticism: Egan's Skills Model of Helping', in Dryden, W. (ed.) *Individual Therapy in Britain*, London, Harper and Row.

Jacques, D. (1984) *Learning in Groups*, London, Croom Helm.

Knowles, M. S. (1975) *Self-Directed Learning: A Guide for Learners and Teachers*, New York, Association Press.

Laurillard, D. (1984), 'Learning from Problem-Solving', in Marton F., Hounsell, D., Entwistle, N. (eds) *The Experience of Learning*, Edinburgh, Scottish Academic Press.

Main, A. (1980) *Encouraging Effective Learning*, Edinburgh, Scottish Academic Press.

Marton, F. (1975) 'What does it take to Learn?' in Entwistle, N. and Hounsell, D. (eds) *How Students Learn*, Lancaster, University of Lancaster.

Marton, F. and Saljo, R. (1984) 'Approaches to Learning', in Marton, F., Hounsell, D., Entwistle, N. (eds) *The Experience of Learning*, Edinburgh, Scottish Academic Press.

Millard, L. (1981) *Adult Learners: Study Skills and Teaching Methods*, University of Nottingham Dept of Adult Education.

Miller, C. M. L. and Parlett, M. (1974) *Up to the Mark: A Study of the Examination Game*, London, Society for Research into Higher Education.

Miller, J. C. (1982) *Tutoring: the Guidance and Counselling Role of the Tutor in vocational preparation*, Hertford, National Institute for Careers Education and Counselling.

More, W. S. (1974) *Emotions and Adult Learning*, Farnborough, Gower.

Murgatroyd, S. (1985) *Counselling and Helping*, London, The British Psychological Society and Methuen.

Nelson-Jones, R. (1982) *The Theory and Practice of Counselling Psychology*, London, Holt, Rinehart and Winston.

Parlett, M. R. (1970) 'The Syllabus-Bound Student', in Hudson, S. (ed.) *The Ecology of Human Intelligence*, Harmondsworth, Penguin.

Pask, G., and Scott, B. C. E. (1972) 'Learning Strategies and Individual Competence', *International Journal of Man-Machine Studies*, vol. 4, pp. 217–53.

Percy K., Butters S., Powell J., and Willett, E. (1983) 'Post-Initial Education in the North West of England: Models of Provision, Barriers to Provision', in Tight, M. (ed), *Education for Adults*, vol. II, *Educational Opportunities for Adults*, London, Croom Helm in association with The Open University.

Perry, W. G. (1970) *Forms of Intellectual and Ethical Development in the College Years: A Scheme*, New York, Holt, Rinehart and Winston.

Powell, J. P. (1981) 'Moving Towards Independent Learning', in Boud, D. (ed.) *Developing Student Autonomy in Learning*, London, Kogan Page.

Ramsden, P., (1979) 'Student Learning and Perceptions of the Academic Environment', *Higher Education*, vol. 8, no. 4, pp. 411–27.

Rhys, S.M. (1981) *Group Work: Notes for a Briefing and Training Session*, Cardiff, The Open University in Wales, mimeo.

Rhys, S.M. (1986) 'Training Student Health Visitors in Helping Skills', in Coping with Crisis Research Group (eds.) *Running Workshops: A Guide for Trainers in the Helping Professions*, London, Croom Helm.

Rhys, S.M. and Lambert, C. (1983), Tutorial Styles and Tutor Assumptions, *Teaching at a Distance*, no. 23, pp. 63–9.

Ruddock, J. (1978) *Learning Through Small Group Discussion*, Guildford, University of Surrey, Society for Research into Higher Education.

Saljo, R. (1979) 'Learning in the Learner's Perspective I: Some Common-sense Conceptions', *Reports from the Department of Education*, University of Goteborg.

Stanton H. (1981) 'Independent Study: A Matter of Confidence', in Boud, D. (ed.) *Developing Student Autonomy in Learning*, London, Kogan Page.

Tough, A. (1971) *The Adult's Learning Projects: a fresh approach to theory and practice in adult learning*, Toronto, Ontario Institute for Studies in Education, Research in Education Series no. 1.

CHAPTER 5: COUNSELLING AT A DISTANCE

Bates, T. (1982) 'Learning From Audio-Visual Media', *Institutional Research Review* 1, pp. 33–57.

British Association for Counselling *et al.* (1984) 'Advice and Counselling Through the Broadcast Media in the United Kingdom', Rugby, B.A.C.

British Broadcasting Corporation (1978 and 1983) *Principles of Counselling*, Series 1 and 2.

Davies, P.G.K. (1982) 'The Functioning of British Counselling Hotlines: A Pilot Study', *British Journal of Guidance and Counselling*, 10, 2 pp. 195–9.

Dryden, W. (ed.) (1984) *Individual Therapy in Britain*, London, Harper and Row.

George, J. (1983) *On The Line: Counselling and Teaching by Telephone* (P519), Milton Keynes, Open University Press.

Glasgow, R.E. and Rosen, G.M. (1978) 'Behavioural Bibliotherapy: A Review of Self-Help Behaviour Therapy Manuals', *Psychological Bulletin*, 85, 1 pp. 1–23.

Hawkins, S. (1985) 'Advice Through Broadcasting: A Question of Standards', *Counselling* 52, pp. 26–30.

Health Education Council (1984) *The Smoker's Guide to Non-Smoking*.

Jacques, D. (1984) *Learning in Groups*, London, Croom Helm, pp. 11–12.

Legge, D. (1982) *The Education of Adults in Britain*, Milton Keynes, Open University Press.

Moore, M. (1981) 'Educational Telephone Networks', *Teaching At a Distance* 19, pp. 24–31.

Oglov, L. (1984) 'Doctors as Radio and Television Hosts: A New Genre of Health Professionals', *Canadian Medical Association Journal*, 130(2) pp. 187–93.

Open University, H. E. C. and Scottish Health Education Unit (1980) *The Good Health Guide*, London, Harper and Row, pp. 98–101.

Open University (1985) *First Year Student Handbook*, Milton Keynes, Open University Press.

Paterson, J. G. and Blashko, C. A. (1984) 'Media Counselling: A New Frontier for Health Professions'. Unpublished paper presented at the 10th International Round Table for the Advancement of Counselling, Aarhus, Denmark. For copy of paper, write to Paterson, Department of Education, University of Alberta, Canada.

Paterson, J. G. and Blashko, C. A. (1986) 'Tentative Answers to a Question of Standards', *Counselling*, Occasional Issue (in press).

Sugarman, L. (1986) 'Counselling and Computers: Introduction and Overview', *British Journal of Guidance and Counselling* 14, 1, pp. 1–11.

Sullivan, T. (1979) *Studying*, Cambridge, National Extension College (Course ED17); *Reading and Understanding* (Course ED18) and *Writing* (Course ED19).

Varah, C. and other Samaritans (1985) *The Samaritans — Refriending the Suicidal*, London, Constable.

Willans A. (1984) 'Counselling?' *Counselling*, 47, Feb, pp. 23–24.

CHAPTER 6: EDUCATIONAL GUIDANCE SERVICES

Adams, J. D., Hayes, J. and Hopson, B. (1976) *Transition: Understanding and Managing Personal Change*, London, Martin Robertson.

Butler, L. (1983) 'Educational Guidance for Adults', in Tight, M. (ed.) *Education for Adults* (Vol 2), London, Croom Helm.

Butler, L. (1984) *Case Studies in Educational Guidance for Adults*, London, National Institute of Adult and Continuing Education and the Advisory Council for Adult and Continuing Education.

Hefferan, J. M., Macy, F. V. and Vickers, D. F. (1976) *Educational Brokering: A New Service for Adult Learners*, New York, National Centre for Educational Brokering.

Hopson, B. and Scally, M. (1984) *Career Builder: a Computer Program For Managing Your Own Career*, Leeds, Life Skills Associates/UHA.

Hopson, B. (1985) 'Adult Life and Career Counselling', *British Journal of Guidance and Counselling*, 13, 1. pp. 49–59.

Hutchinson, E. and Hutchinson, E. (1978) *Learning Later: Fresh Horizons in English Adult Education*, London, Routledge and Kegan Paul.

Legge D. (1982) *The Education of Adults in Britain*, Milton Keynes, Open University Press.

Murgatroyd, S. and Redmond, M. (1978) 'Collaborative Adult Education Counselling: Models and Practices', *Teaching At A Distance* 13, pp. 18–26.

Sewart, D. (1981) 'Distance Teaching: A Contradiction in Terms?', *Teaching At A Distance* 19, pp. 8–18.

Super, D.E. (1957) *The Psychology of Careers*, New York, Harper and Row.

Watts, A.G. (1980a) 'Educational and Careers Guidance Services for Adults I: A Rationale and Conceptual Framework', *British Journal of Guidance and Counselling*, 8, 1, pp. 11–22.

Watts, A.G. (1980b) 'Educational and Careers Guidance Services for Adults II: A Review of Current Provision', *British Journal of Guidance and Counselling*, 8, 2, pp. 188–202.

Watts, A.G. (1981) 'Introduction' in Watts A.G., Super D.E. and Kidd J.M. (eds) *Careers Development in Britain*, Cambridge, Hobsons Press.

CHAPTER 7: COUNSELLING AND WORK

Closs, S.J. (1986) 'Current and Future Developments of the JIIG-CAL System', *British Journal of Guidance and Counselling*, 14(1), pp. 53–65.

Cooper, C.L. and Davidson, M. (1982) *High Pressure — Working Lives of Women Managers*, London, Fontana.

Crocker, O., Charney, C. and Chiu, J.S.L. (1984) *Quality Circles — A Guide to Participation and Productivity*, Toronto, Methuen.

Gilbert, G. (1977) 'The Role of the Professional Counsellor', in Watts, A.G. (ed.) *Counselling at Work*, London, Bedford Square Press.

Ginzberg, E., Ginzburg, S.W., Axelrad, S. and Herma, J.L. (1951) *Occupational Choice — An Approach to a General Theory*, New York, Columbia University Press.

Harris-Bowlsbey, J. (1984) 'The Computer as a Tool in Careers Guidance Programmes', in Gysbers, N.C. and Associates (eds) *Designing Careers*, San Francisco, Jossey-Bass.

Heppner, M.J. (1985) 'Discover II, SIGI and Microskills — A Descriptive Review', *Journal of Counselling and Development*, 63(5), pp. 323–5.

Hill, J.M.M. (1969) *Transition from School to Work*, London, Tavistock Institute for Human Relations.

Hood, V., Hollingsworth, A. and Bannister, J. (1977) 'Counselling within Other Roles', in Watts, A.G. (ed.) *Counselling at Work*, London, Bedford Square Press.

Hopson, B. (1977) 'Setting up a Counselling Network', in Watts, A.G. (ed.) *Counselling at Work*, London, Bedford Square Press.

Hopson, B. (1985) 'Adult Life and Career Counselling', *British Journal of Guidance and Counselling*, 13(1), pp. 49–59.

Hopson, B. and Scally, M. (1984) *Career Builder — A Computer Program for Managing Your Own Career*, Leeds, Lifeskills Associates/UHA.

Howard, R.W. *'Coping and Adapting*, London, Angus Robertson.

Katz, M.R. (1984) 'Computer Assisted Guidance — A Walkthrough with Running Comments, *Journal of Counselling and Development*, 63(3), pp. 153–7.

Kuhn, A. and Wolpe, M. (eds) (1978) *Feminism and Materialism — Women and Modes of Production*, London, Routledge and Kegan Paul.

Law, W.M. and Watts, A.G. (1977) *Schools, Careers and Community*, London, Church Information Office.

McDonald, N. and Doyle, M. (1981) *The Stress of Work*, London, Nelson.

Murgatroyd, S. (1985) *Counselling and Helping*, London, British Psychological Society and Methuen.

Peters, T. and Waterman, R.H. (1982) *In Search of Excellence*, London, Harper and Row.

Pyle, K.R. (1984) 'Career Counselling and Computers — Where's the Creativity?', *Journal of Counselling and Development*, 63(3), pp. 141–4.

Sampson, J.P. (1984) 'The Use of Computers', in Burck, H.D. and Reardon, R.C., (eds) *Career Development Interventions*, Springfield, Illinois, Charles C. Thomas.

Sheehy, G. (1982) *Pathfinders — How to Achieve Happiness by Conquering Life's Crises*, London, Sidgwick and Jackson.

Smart, C. and Smart, B. (eds) (1978) *Women, Sexuality and Social Control*, London, Routledge and Kegan Paul.

Strong, E.K. and Campbell, D.P. (1977) *Manual for the Strong-Campbell Interest Inventory*, Stanford, California: Stanford University Press.

Super, D.E. (1957) *The Psychology of Careers*, New York, Harper and Row.

Super, D.E., Kidd, J.M. and Watts, A.G. (1977) *The Career Development Inventory (UK)*, Cambridge, National Institute for Careers Education and Counselling (mimeo).

Sworder, G. (1977) 'Counselling Problems at Work', in Watts, A.G. (ed.) *Counselling at Work*, London, Bedford Square Press.

Veness, T. (1962) *School Leavers — Their Aspirations and Expectations*, London, Methuen.

Warshaw, M.D. (1979) *Managing Stress*, Reading, Mass, Addison-Wesley.

Watts, A.G. and Ballantine, M. (1983) 'Computers in Careers Guidance — The British Experience', *Counselling Psychologist*, 11(4), pp. 49–59.

Watts, A.G., Law, W.M. and Fawcett, B. (1981) 'Some Implications for Guidance Practice', in Watts, A.G., Super, D.E. and Kidd, J.M. (eds) *Career Development in Britain*, Cambridge, Careers Research and Advisory Centre.

Williams, W.M. (ed.) (1974) *Occupational Choice*, London, Allen and Unwin.

Willis, P. (1972) *Learning to Labour — How Working Class Kids get Working Class Jobs*, London, Saxon House.

CHAPTER 8: COUNSELLING FOR UNEMPLOYMENT AND RETIREMENT

Atchley, R.C. (1976) *The Social Forces in Later Life — An Introduction to Social Gerontology*, 2nd edition, Belmont, Wadsworth.

Cobb, S. and Kassl, S. (1977) *Termination — The Consequences of Job Loss*, Cincinatti, United States Department of Health, Education and Welfare.

Corey, G. and Corey, M.S. (1977) *Groups — Processes and Practices*, Monteray, Brooks-Cole.

Davis, M. Eshelman, E.R. and McKay, M. (1980) *The Relaxation and Stress Reduction Workbook*, Richmond, Calif. New Harbinger Publications.

Douglas, T. (1968) *Groupwork*, London, Tavistock Institute for Human Relations.

Dryden, W. (1984) 'Rational Emotive Psychotherapy', in Dryden, W. (ed.) *Individual Psychotherapy in Britain*, London, Harper and Row.

Frankl, V.E. (1978) *The Unheard Cry for Meaning — Psychotherapy and Humanism*, New York, Washington Square Press.

Gazda, G.M. (1978) *Group Counselling — A Developmental Approach* 2nd edition, Boston, Allyn and Bacon.

Gershuny, J.I. (1978) *After Industrial Society — The Emerging Self-Service Economy*, London, Macmillan.

Golan, N. (1981) *Passing Through Transitions — A Guide for Practitioners*, New York, Free Press.

Jacobson, G.R. and Lindsay, D. (1979) 'Screening of Alcohol Problems Among The Unemployed', *Current Alcohol Research*, vol. 7, pp. 357–71.

Jacques, D. (1984) *Learning in Groups*, London, Croom Helm.

Kelvin, P. (1981) 'Work as a Source of Identity — The Implications of Unemployment', *British Journal of Guidance and Counselling*, vol. 9(1), pp. 2–11.

Kleemeier, R.W. (1975) 'Leisure and Disengagement in Retirement', in Sze, W.C. (ed.) *The Human Life Cycle*, New York, Jason Aronson.

Lakein, A. (1973) *How to Get Control of Your Time and Your Life*, New York, Signet Books.

Lange, A.J. and Jakubowski, P. (1980) *Responsible Assertive Behaviour — Cognitive/Behavioural Procedures for Trainers*, Champaign, Illinois, Research Press.

Marsden, D. (1982) *Workless — An Exploration of the Social Contract between Society and the Worker*, London, Croom Helm.

Marsden, D. and Duff, E. (1975) *Workless — Some Unemployed Men and their Families*, Harmondsworth, Penguin.

Murgatroyd, S. (1985a) *Counselling and Helping*, London, British Psychological Society/Methuen Books.

Murgatroyd, S. (1985b) 'Dealing with an Acute Crisis in Marital Relationships', in Dryden, W. (ed.) *Marital Therapy in Britain*, vol. 2. London, Harper and Row.

Murgatroyd, S. (1982) 'Coping and the Crisis Counsellor', *British Journal of Guidance and Counselling*, vol. 10(2), pp. 220–8.

Murgatroyd, S. and Shooter, M. (1982) *Unemployment, The Person and the Family*, The Open University in Wales, Coping with Crisis Research Group, (mimeo).

Murgatroyd, S. and Woolfe, R. (1985) *Helping Families in Distress — An Introduction to Family Focused Helping*, London, Harper and Row.

Murgatroyd, S. and Woolfe, R. (1982) *Coping with Crisis — Understanding and Helping People in Need*, London, Harper and Row.

Murray-Parkes, C. (1972) *Bereavement: Studies of Grief in Adult Life*, Harmondsworth, Penguin.

Pahl, R. E. (1980) 'Employment, Work and the Domestic Division of Labour', *International Journal of Urban and Regional Research*, vol. 4(1), pp. 16–36.

Peters, T. and Austin, N. (1985) *A Passion for Excellence — The Leadership Difference*, London, Collins.

Rice, M. S. (1981) *Working Class Wives — Their Health and Conditions*, London, Virago. (*First published in 1939*.,)

Roberts, K., Duggan, J. and Noble, M. (1982) 'Out of School Youth in High Unemployment Areas — An Empirical Investigation', *British Journal of Guidance and Counselling*, vol. 10(1), pp. 1–11.

Schlossberg, N. K. and Leibowitz, Z. (1980) 'Organizational Support Systems as Buffers to Job Loss', *Journal of Vocational Behaviour*, vol. 17, pp. 204–17.

Schwartz, S. L. (1971) 'A Review of Crisis Intervention Programmes', *Psychiatric Quarterly*, vol. 45(4), pp. 498–508.

Seligman, M. E. P. (1974) 'Depression and Learned Helplessness', in Friedman, R. J. and Katz, M. M. (eds) *The Psychology of Depression — Contemporary Theory and Research*. Washington, Winston-Wiley.

Shooter, M. S. (1986) 'Workshops on Death and Dying', in Coping with Crisis Research Group, Open University (eds) *Running Workshops — A Guide for Trainers in the Helping Professions*, London, Croom Helm.

Smart, C. and Smart, B. (eds) *Women, Sexuality and Social Control*, London, Routledge and Kegan Paul.

Smart, R. G. (1979) 'Drinking Problems Amongst Employed, Unemployed and Shift Workers', *Journal of Medicine*, vol. 21(11), pp. 731–6.

Watts, A. G. (1981) 'Careers Education and the Informal Economies', *British Journal of Guidance and Counselling*,. vol. 9(1), pp. 24–35.

Woodcock, M. (1979) *Team Development Manual*, Hants, UK, Gower.

Zaretsky, E. (1971) *Capitalism, The Family and Personal Life*, London, Pluto Press.

ENDPIECE

ACACE (1982) *Continuing Education: From Policies to Practise*, Leicester, ACACE.

ACSTT (1975) *Advisory Committee on the Training of Teachers for Further Education*, London, ACSTT.

ACSTT (1978) *The Training of Adult Education Part-time Further Education Teachers*, London, ACSTT.

Elsden, K.T. (1975) *Training for Adult Education*, University of Nottingham and NIAE, Nottingham.

Miller, J. (1982) *Tutoring: The Guidance and Counselling Role of the Tutor in Vocational Preparation*, Further Education Curriculum Review and Development Unit.

Murgatroyd, S. (1982) 'Experiential Learning and the Person in Pursuit of Psychology', *Education Section Review, British Psychological Society*, vol. 6, no. 2, pp. 112–17.

16+ Scottish Action Plan: (1983) *16–18 in Scotland: An Action Plan*, Scottish Education Department, HMSO.

Woolfe, R. (1986) 'Experiential Learning in Work-shops', Ch. 1. (eds.) COPING WITH CRISIS RESEARCH GROUP. *Running Workshops: A Guide for Trainers in the Helping Professions*, Beckenham, Croom Helm.

Name Index

Subject Index